莲花盛开
庆祝澳门回归二十周年

BLOOMING LOTUS FLOWER
20th Anniversary of Macao's Return

汪灵犀 撰文
WANG LINGXI

中国画报出版社·北京
China Pictorial Press·Beijing

图书在版编目（CIP）数据

莲花盛开：庆祝澳门回归二十周年：汉英对照 / 汪灵犀撰文；钟丽莎译. —— 北京：中国画报出版社，2019.12

ISBN 978-7-5146-1834-1

Ⅰ. ①莲… Ⅱ. ①汪… ②钟… Ⅲ. ①澳门问题—画册 Ⅳ. ①D829.12-64

中国版本图书馆CIP数据核字(2019)第252924号

莲花盛开：庆祝澳门回归二十周年

汪灵犀 撰文　钟丽莎 译

出 版 人：	于九涛
出版统筹：	方允仲
执行策划：	王 辉
特约编辑：	孙恩光　梁树森　马志毅
责任编辑：	刘晓雪
中文定稿：	王亚明（特邀）
英文编辑：	王国振　陈 旭
英文改稿：	迈克尔·杰佛里·默里
英文校对：	朱露茜
设　　计：	敖艳超
责任印制：	焦 洋

出版发行：	中国画报出版社
地　　址：	中国北京市海淀区车公庄西路33号　邮编：100048
发 行 部：	010-68469781　010-68414683（传真）
总 编 室：	010-88417359　版权部：010-88417359
开　　本：	16开（889mm×1194mm）
印　　张：	11.5
字　　数：	100千字
版　　次：	2019年12月第1版　2019年12月第1次印刷
印　　刷：	北京汇瑞嘉合文化发展有限公司
书　　号：	ISBN 978-7-5146-1834-1
定　　价：	380.00元

SUPPORTED BY

Government Information Bureau of Macao SAR

General Department of Publicity and Culture of Liaison Office of the Central People's Government in the Macao SAR

PHOTOS CONTRIBUTED BY

Liaison Office of the Central People's Government in the Macao SAR

Government Information Bureau of Macao SAR

Region People's Liberation Army Macao Garrison

Xinhua News Agency

China News Service

Visual China Group

Cloud Land Photography

PHOTOS COURTESY OF

Isaac Lawrence

Li Rurong

Zhang Ziliang

Zhao Cunye

支持单位

澳门特别行政区政府新闻局

中央人民政府驻澳门特别行政区联络办公室宣传文化部

图片提供

中央人民政府驻澳门特别行政区联络办公室

澳门特别行政区政府新闻局

中国人民解放军驻澳门部队

新华通讯社

中国新闻社

视觉中国

澳门云上摄影有限公司

艾萨克·劳伦斯

李汝荣

张子量

赵村野

前言

2019年，澳门回归20周年。

从1553年葡萄牙人强行侵占到1999年正式回归，440多年的时间里，澳门这片土地历尽沧桑。

如今的澳门已是风华正茂，旅游、经济、治安、教育等各方面的飞速发展让澳门生机勃勃，澳门未来发展空间广阔。

回归20年来，在中央政府的坚强领导下，在澳门特别行政区政府和澳门同胞的共同努力下，澳门保持了良好的发展态势，经济平稳增长，社会和谐稳定，居民安居乐业。澳门走上了同祖国内地优势互补、共同发展的宽广道路，"一国两制"实践取得举世公认的成功。

回归后，澳门是全世界经济增长速度最快的地区之一，澳门的人均GDP也是全世界最高的地区之一；澳门居民的生活幸福指数很高，从2007年开始，澳门就已经推行了从幼儿园到高中的15年义务教育，澳门的免费医疗被世界卫生组织评为"太平洋地区典范"……在"一国两制"的实践上，澳门地位重要，独具特色，亮点不少，被视为"模范生"。

新时代下，澳门又迎来一系列重大发展机遇。粤港澳大湾区建设，泛珠三角区域合作，"一带一路"倡议，中葡经贸合作等平台，为澳门发展绘就了壮丽的蓝图。"大河中流下，青山两岸移。"在中央政府的大力支持和澳门特别行政区政府与社会各界的共同努力下，澳门这朵植根于祖国大地的金莲花，正在南海之滨迎风盛开，芳香四溢。

PREFACE

The year 2019 marks the 20th anniversary of Macao's return to the motherland.

During the approximately 440 years from the invasion to the Portuguese in 1553 to its return to the motherland in 1999, Macao underwent various vicissitudes. Today, it is enjoying a prime time, with booming tourism, rapid economic development, good public security and a flourishing education cause. Its society is full of vigor, seeing a promising future.

Over the past 20 years since Macao's return, under the strong leadership of the Central Government and with the joint efforts of the government and people of the Special Administrative Region (SAR), Macao has maintained a good development trend, enjoying steady economic growth and social harmony and stability. Its citizens live and work in peace and contentment. It has embarked on a promising path of mutual complementarity and common development with the Chinese hinterland. The implementation of the "one country, two systems" in Macao has proven a universally acknowledged success.

Macao's economic growth rate is one of the fastest in the world, and its per-capita GDP is also one of the highest. Macao residents have a high index of happiness in regard to their lives. Since 2007, Macao has been able to implementing a 15-year compulsory education system from kindergarten to senior high school. Its free medical care has been rated by the WHO as a "Model in the Pacific Region". In the practice of "one country, two systems", Macao holds an important position with unique features and many highlights, regarded as a "model" for use elsewhere.

In the new era, Macao has also ushered in a range of important opportunities for development. Construction of the Guangdong-Hong Kong-Macao Greater Bay Area, Pan-Pearl River Delta regional cooperation, Belt and Road Initiative, and the Sino-Portuguese economic and trade cooperation platform combine to create a grand blueprint for further development. There is an old saying that "the boat moves downstream through the rapids, and green mountains flanking the river recede". With the full support of the Central Government and the joint efforts of the government and people from various sectors in Macao, the globeflower rooted in the rich soil of the motherland is in full bloom alongside the South China Sea.

目录

001 第一章 游子归家 拥抱祖国
百年夙愿，吐气扬眉终酬成真

023 第二章 "一国两制" 澳人治澳
背靠祖国，濠江小城快速成长

059 第三章 善抓机遇 经济飞跃
依托内地，小舞台上演大戏码

101 第四章 中西荟萃 包容共济
幸福和谐，多元文化生机勃发

157 第五章 凝心聚力 续谱新篇
未来可期，澳门的明天会更好

CONTENTS

001   I.   **Macao Returns to the Embrace of the Motherland**
Long-cherished Wish Finally Achieved

023   II.   **One Country, Two Systems, Macao People Governing Macao**
With the Support of the Motherland, the Small City by the Haojiang River Grows Rapidly

059   III.   **Achieving Leapfrog Economic Development by Seizing the Opportunities in a Timely Way**
Depending on the Hinterland to Put on a Big Play on a Small Stage

101   IV.   **An Inclusive City with Combined Chinese and Western Styles**
A Happy and Harmonious Home Featuring Vital Multi-Culture

157   V.   **Making Joint Efforts to Write a New Chapter**
Looking forward to a Bright Future

第一章

游子归家 拥抱祖国

百年夙愿，吐气扬眉终盼成真

I.
Macao Returns to the Embrace of the Motherland

Long-cherished Wish Finally Achieved

002 莲花盛开
BLOOMING LOTUS FLOWER

你可知"妈港"不是我的真名姓？……
我离开你的襁褓太久了，母亲！
但是他们掳去的是我的肉体，你依然保管着我内心的灵魂。
三百年来梦寐不忘的生母啊！
请叫儿的乳名，叫我一声"澳门"！
母亲！我要回来，母亲！

这是闻一多先生写的一首充满了爱国情怀的诗。《诗经》中的《凯风》一诗，其子七人自怨自艾。1925年闻一多借以为题，作《七子之歌》，咏叹这些地方似有儿女脱离母亲，澳门便是其中之一。

澳门，自古是中国领土，然而从16世纪中叶开始，逐步被葡萄牙非法占领。中华人民共和国成立后，中国政府曾多次阐明澳门是中国的领土，主张在适当时候通过谈判和平解决历史遗留问题。

一个不可逆转的历史进程从1987年开始，这一年的4月13日，中葡联合声明在北京正式签署，向全世界严正宣告中国将于1999年12月20日对澳门恢复行使主权。这个饱经外漂泊了400多年的游子，终于踏上归家行程。

1993年3月31日，全国人大通过了经广泛征询和吸收澳人意见制定的《澳门特别行政区基本法》，"一国两制"伟大构想以法律形式落定成型。以此为起点，澳门开始了过渡期的各项准备和推进工作。广大澳门同胞焕发扬爱祖国、爱澳门的优良传统，团结一致，携手奋斗，保持了澳门社会的稳定，促进了澳门经济的发展，社会各界对澳门前途的信心大为增强。

1999年12月20日零时，当回归的钟声敲响，鲜艳的五星红旗在澳门上空冉冉升起，莲花区旗第一次在澳门迎风飘扬，数万名群众在广东海珠拱北口岸广场，用鲜花和掌声热烈欢送中国人民解放军铁甲雄师赴澳门执行新的使命，全体中华民族与有荣焉。

从宏伟的天安门广场到偏僻的小山村，从与澳门山水相连的珠海到远隔重洋的异国他乡，亿万双中华儿女的眼睛都在见证这历史性一刻，释放心中一片深情。钟声之后，中华儿女把所有的屈辱丢进夜的黑暗，把对明天的希望注入灿烂的黎明。

百年风愿，九九归一。在澳门回归祖国的历史进程中，我们有辛酸和泪水，有不屈和奋争，更有扬眉吐气的自豪。澳门被占领，是旧中国积贫积弱的命运使然；澳门回到祖国怀抱，则是新中国日益繁荣昌盛的必然结果。澳门回归祖国，揭开了历史新的一页，祖国富强一日千里，澳门未来灿烂光明。

004 莲花盛开 BLOOMING LOTUS FLOWER

Do you know that "Ma Kwok" is not my real name?

I've left your swaddling clothes for too long, Mother!

But what they have taken away is my flesh, and you still have my soul.

Mother whom I have never forgotten day and night!

Please call me by my infant name, call me "Ao Men"!

Mother! I want to come back, Mother!

This is part of the patriotic poem *Song of the Seven Sons*, written by Mr. Wen Yiduo (Wen I-to). According to the poem entitled *Kaifeng* in ancient *Book of Songs*, a mother of seven sons in the ancient State of Chenshucun laments the existing state of chaos while her seven sons bemoan their unhappy fate. In 1926, Wen Yiduo chose seven Chinese places occupied by imperialist powers to compose this poem, and Macao was one of them.

Macao has been part of China since ancient times. However, it fell into the hands of Portuguese colonialism in the mid-16th Century. After the founding of the People's Republic of China in October 1949, the Chinese Government repeatedly stated that Macao was part of China, and proposed to peacefully settle the historical issues through negotiations at an appropriate time.

An irreversible historical process began in 1987. On April 13 of that year, the Sino-Portuguese Joint Declaration was officially signed in Beijing, solemnly proclaiming to the world that China would resume its sovereignty over Macao on December 20, 1999. Thus, the son who had been absent from home for over 400 years was finally making the journey back.

On March 31, 1993, the National People's Congress (NPC) China's top legislature, approved the Basic Law of the Macao SAR, which was enacted after extensive consultations and fully considering Macao people's opinions. The great concept of "one country, two systems" was finalized in the form of law. Then, Macao set out to make various preparations and promote relevant work in the transition period. Macao compatriots carried forward the fine tradition of loving the motherland and loving Macao, and worked hard together to maintain social stability and promote economic development. People from all sectors in Macao had greater confidence in its future.

When the bell celebrating Macao's return rang out at zero hour on December 20, 1999, the bright Five-Starred Red Flag rose slowly over the regained land, and the Macao SAR Flag with five stars, lotus flower, bridge and sea water fluttered in the wind there for the first time. At Gongbei Port Square in Zhuhai, in neighboring Guangdong Province, tens of thousands of people saw off the PLA soldiers with flowers and applause as they departed for their new mission in Macao. The whole Chinese nation took pride of this grand event.

From the grandeur of Tian'anmen Square in Beijing to remote small mountain villages, and from Zhuhai, adjoining Macao, to foreign lands on the other side of the ocean, millions upon millions of Chinese people witnessed this historic moment, and expressed their deep feelings. After the bell struck, the Chinese people cast off all the historic disgrace long endured and looked forward to a bright future.

From the grandeur of Tian'anmen Square in Beijing to remote small mountain villages, and from Zhuhai, adjoining Macao, to foreign lands on the other side of the ocean, millions upon millions of Chinese people witnessed this historic moment, and expressed their deep feelings. After the bell struck, the Chinese people cast off all the historic disgrace long endured and looked forward to a bright future.

1987年3月26日上午，澳门居民在街道电器商店的电视机前观看卫星转播中葡关于澳门问题的联合声明在北京草签仪式

On the morning of Marched 26, 1987, Macao citizens watched the ceremony of initialing the Sino-Portuguese Joint Declaration on Macao in Beijing via satellite broadcasting in front of a street electrical apparatus shop.

1987年4月14日，代表们举手通过关于授权全国人大常委会审议批准关于澳门问题的联合声明的决定

On April 14, 1987, representatives held up for authorizing NPC Standing Committee to examine and approve the Joint Declaration of the Government of People's Republic of China and the Government of the Republic of Portugal on the Question of Macao.

澳门基本法颁布后,澳门各界举办了多种形式的宣传、推广基本法的活动。1996年5月30日,《中华人民共和国澳门特别行政区基本法》正式发布于国际互联网。图为澳门基本法协进会代表和澳门电讯公司的代表在签署上网协议

After the promulgation of The Basic Law of the Macao Special Administrative Region of the People's Republic of China, Macao organized various activities to publicize and promote its implementation. On May 30, 1996, it was officially published on the Internet. The picture shows the signing of the access agreement between representatives of the Macao Association for the Advancement of the Basic Law and the Telecoms Corporation of Macao.

008 莲花盛开
BLOOMING LOTUS FLOWER

1999年5月6日，根据中国国家标准制作的中国国旗、国徽与澳门特区区旗、区徽在澳门亮相
On May 6, 1999, the PRC National Flag and Emblem manufactured according to Chinese national standards, and the Macao SAR flag along with its emblem appeared in Macao.

1999年10月8日上午,"粤港澳海(水)警迎澳门回归联合演习"在澳门和珠海对开海面上举行

A shot of the Guangdong-Hong Kong-Macao Marine Police Welcoming Macao's Return on the sea between Macao and Zhuhai on the morning of October 8, 1999.

1999年10月31日，一些澳门儿童在街头挥舞中华人民共和国国旗与澳门特别行政区区旗，庆祝澳门回归倒计时五十天

On October 31, 1999, Macao children waved the PRC National Flag and the flag of the Macao SAR in the streets to celebrate the fifty-day countdown to Macao's return.

1999年10月31日，"99迎澳门回归环山行"活动在澳门松山举行，来自新华社澳门分社、外交部澳门办事处以及在澳门的30家中资公司的1300多人参加了这次环山步行

On October 31, 1999, the Macao-Return Round-the-Mountain Trip was held in Songshan of Macao. More than 1,300 participants came from the Macao Branch of Xinhua News Agency, the Macao Office of the Ministry of Foreign Affairs and 30 Chinese-funded companies in Macao.

莲花盛开
BLOOMING LOTUS FLOWER

1999年12月9日，与珠海至澳门的莲花大桥配套的设施"横琴口岸"通过验收
On December 9, 1999, Hengqin Port, a support facility of the Zhuhai-Macao Lotus Bridge, passed its national acceptance test.

1999年12月11日，为迎接澳门回归，珠海拱北口岸进行了全面整修装饰，口岸夜景流光溢彩，十分漂亮
On December 11, 1999, Gongbei Port of Zhuhai was renovated and decorated in an all-round way to welcome the return of Macao. The night scenery of the port was brilliant and beautiful.

1999年12月15日，知名歌手牟玄甫和曲比阿乌正在为澳门回归庆典文艺晚会排演《牡丹之歌》

On December 15, 1999, an evening gala celebrated Macao's return to the embrace of the motherland. The performers included famous singers Mou Xuanfu and Qubi Awu, seen here rehearsing The Song of Peony.

1999年12月17日，上海市侨联举行"庆祝澳门回归，迎接2000年"文艺汇演，一千多名侨界人士及港澳同胞济济一堂，共同抒发对澳门回归祖国的喜悦之情

On December 17, 1999, the Shanghai Overseas Chinese Federation organized a literary and artistic performance - Celebrating Macao's Return and Welcoming the Year 2000. More than 1,000 overseas Chinese and their compatriots and relatives from Hong Kong and Macao expressed their joy at Macao's return to the motherland.

1999年12月17日,澳门小歌手陆劲东、陈芷华在北京加紧排练,准备20日晚在北京首都体育馆举行的"首都各届庆祝澳门回归祖国大会"上演出

On December 17, 1999, Macao singers Lu Jindong and Chen Zhihua rehearsed in Beijing in preparation for the evening party held to celebrate Macao's return on December 20.

1999年12月19日，中国人民解放军三军仪仗队进入澳门政权交接大厅，执行盛典礼仪任务

On December 19, 1999, the honor guard of the three armed forces of the Chinese People's Liberation Army entered the site of the handover of Macao to perform the grand ceremony.

1999年12月20日零时，北京天安门广场澳门回归倒计时牌前一片欢腾

At 0:00 on December 20, 1999, jubilation erupted in Tian'anmen Square in Beijing as the countdown card for Macao's return reached zero.

1999年12月20日,驻澳部队经珠海进入澳门

On December 20, 1999, the PLA garrison troops went into Macao through Zhuhai.

1999年12月20日回归日清晨,中国银行澳门分行在中银大厦广场举行升旗仪式

On the morning of December 20, 1999, the day Macao returned home, the Bank of China Macao Branch held a solemn flag-raising ceremony in the Plaza of the Bank of China Building.

1999年12月20日中午,在欢迎解放军入城后,澳门各界庆祝澳门回归祖国活动委员会举办"迈向美好明天大巡游"活动。澳门居民走上街头,争睹大巡游盛况。

At noon on December 20, 1999, after welcoming the PLA garrison entering Macao, the Macao's Committee for Activities to Celebrate Macao's Return to the Motherland held a "Grand Tour Towards a Better Tomorrow". Macao citizens and their families thronged the streets to witness the grand parade.

第二章
"一国两制" 澳人治澳

背靠祖国，濠江小城快速成长

II.
One Country,
Two Systems,
Macao People
Governing Macao

With the Support of the Motherland,
the Small City by the Haojiang
River Grows Rapidly

回归后,澳门最大的变化表现在哪里?不少澳门人会告诉你,是站起来、富起来的精神面貌和主人翁的风采。

1999年5月15日,澳门特别行政区第一届政府推选委员会依法选举产生了第一任行政长官,这是"一国两制""澳人治澳""高度自治"的重要实践,是有史以来,澳门人民第一次当家作主。

"这一票的分量好重啊!"当行政长官选举结果公布的那一瞬间,会议大厅里掌声雷动,许多人哽咽着说不出话来。

几百年来,澳门人受尽屈辱,连自己的母语都不能在正式场合使用,祖居澳门的中国人没有任何权利可言。这一切从行政长官人选公布的那一刻起得到根本改变:190多名推选委员的掌声,宣告澳门同胞已经直起腰板,堂堂正正地登上了政治舞台。澳门人自己当家作主的时代开始了!

1999年10月12日,澳门特区第一届立法会举行了第一次全体会议,通过无记名投票方式选举出主席、副主席等人选。忠于职守,为澳门社会的繁荣稳定、"一国两制"的成功实践努力,为澳门居民做更多、更好的事,成为大多数议员的共同心声。20年末,特区立法会共制定和修改了包括《维护国家安全法》《立法法》《土地法》《城市规划法》在内的200多部法律,"法治"在澳门治理中日益制度化、程序化,特区政府在立法会的监督下依法施政。

2000年3月,澳门12月20日回归当天,外交部驻澳门特派员公署开署。2011年,国家"十二五"规划港澳部分首次独立成章,参与国家整体战略高度,为澳门经济发展指明了方向,提供了新的机遇和发展空间。

党的十八大以来,以习近平同志为核心的党中央系澳门同胞,将"一国两制"实践有机融入实现中华民族大复兴中国梦的宏图伟业之中,推动"一国两制"事业取得新的进展。

2013年,澳门大学新校区在珠海横琴岛落成启用,澳门大学实现了"有校园"的大学梦;同样在横琴开发区,一个占地5平方公里的粤澳合作产业园,孕育着各项新兴产业;地域狭小是制约澳门发展的"老大难"问题,2015年,国务院划定澳门85平方公里的水域管理范围和陆地界限,给澳门发展预留下充足空间;2018年,港珠澳大桥正式通车运营,这座"惊天飞龙"跨越了天堑,联通了人心;2019年,粤港澳大湾区发展规划纲要全文公布,为澳门带来前所未有的发展机会……

与此同时,澳门的国际影响力不断提升。2005年10月29日,第四届东亚运动会一连9天在澳门举行,共9个国家及地区派出近2000名运动员,参加17个大项的比赛。2008年5月3日,120位火炬手经3小时接力传递,北京奥运圣火历史性地走进澳门大街小巷,25万居民和游客夹道欢迎圣火。截至目前,澳门以"中国澳门"名义在世界10多个国际组织享有单独地位,有近百个国家在澳门设有领事馆或开展领事业务……

回归以来,在中央政府和内地的大力支持下,在特区政府和历任行政长官的带领下,"一国两制""澳人治澳""高度自治"取得了丰硕成果,澳门特区政府运作顺畅,各级公务员履职尽责,民主化、公开化的程度前所未有。

作为一项前所未有的伟大实践,"一国两制"事业还需要不断探索推进,但我们始终对未来充满信心。"无论遇到什么样的困难和挑战,我们推进'一国两制'方针的信心和决心都绝不会动摇,实践'一国两制'的信心和决心都绝不会动摇。"这就是时代的强音。

What are the biggest changes in Macao after its return? Many Macao people said they had finally stood up, got rich and became the masters of Macao.

On May 15, 1999, the 1st Chief Executive was elected by the initial representative election committee of the Macao SAR in accordance with the law, which was an important practice of the principle of "one country, two systems", "Macao people governing Macao" enjoying a high degree of autonomy. It marked a great turning point for the people of Macao to become their own masters.

"What a heavy vote!" When the result of the Chief Executive's election was announced, the conference hall was filled with a storm of applause, and many people choked and couldn't speak.

For hundreds of years, Macao people had been humiliated, not even allowed to use their mother tongue on official occasions. The Chinese whose ancestors lived in Macao for generations had no rights. However, everything changed fundamentally from the moment when the result of the Chief Executive's election was announced. The applause of more than 190 representative election committee members showed that Macao compatriots had stood tall and stepped onto the political stage in a dignified manner. The local people ushered in a new era of administering Macao themselves.

On October 12 of the same year, the 1st Legislative Assembly of the Macao SAR held its initial plenary meeting, electing chairman, vice-chairmen and other members by secret ballot. It was the common aspiration of most members to devote themselves to their duties, working hard for the social prosperity and stability of Macao and promoting the successful practice of "one country, two systems" and do more for their compatriots. In the past two decades, the Legislative Assembly of the Macao SAR has enacted and revised more than 200 laws, including the Law on Maintaining National Security, Legislation Law, Land Law and Urban Planning Law. Macao was increasingly placed under the rule of law through institutionalization and procedures. The SAR government exercises administration according to law under supervision of the Legislative Assembly.

On December 20, the day Macao returned to the embrace of the motherland, the Office of the Commissioner of the Ministry of Foreign Affairs of the People's Republic of China in the Macao Special Administrative Region was opened. In March of the following year, Macao sent its independent deputies to attend the "two sessions" [the National People's Congress and the Chinese People's Political

Consultative Committee] to fully participate in national affairs. In 2011, the 12th Five-Year Plan had a separate chapter relating to Hong Kong and Macao. This set a direction for Macao's economic development in the overall national strategy, and provided new opportunities and development space for Macao, enabling it to gradually become integrated into the overall deployment of national development.

Since the 18th National Congress of the Communist Party of China (CPC) in 2012, the CPC Central Committee with Xi Jinping as the core always shown its concern for Macao compatriots, organically integrating the practice of "one country, two systems" into the "Chinese Dream" of great national rejuvenation, which helped promote the cause of "one country, two systems" for further rapid progress.

In 2013, the new campus of the University of Macau was completed and opened in Hengqin of Zhuhai, realizing the university's dream of having a real "home". An industrial park of cooperation between Guangdong and Macao, covering an area of five square km, in the Hengqin Economic Development Zone cultivated various emerging industries. The limited area under its control was a historic major factor restricting development of Macao. In 2015, the State Council delineated the boundaries of its water and land area covering 85 square km, reserving sufficient space for expanded development. In 2018, the Hong Kong-Zhuhai-Macao Bridge was officially opened to traffic, enabling people in the three areas to become much closer to each other. In 2019, the development plan for the Guangdong-Hong Kong-Macao Greater Bay Area was promulgated, bringing unprecedented opportunities.

Meanwhile, the international influence of Macao has been increasing continuously. On October 29, 2005, the 4th East Asian Games was held in Macao over nine days, with 17 events attended by about 2,000 athletes from nine countries and regions. Through a three-hour torch relay by 120 torchbearers on May 3, 2008, the sacred flame of the Beijing Olympics was carried throughout Macao, welcomed by 250,000 residents and many tourists lining the streets. So far, Macao has enjoyed separate representation in over 10 international organizations in the name of "Macao China", and some 100 countries have set up consulates or provided consular services there.

With vigorous support from the Central Government and the hinterland and under the leadership of the SAR Government and all the chief executives since its return, fruitful results have been achieved in the cause of "one country, two systems", "Macao people governing Macao" and enjoying a high degree of autonomy. Macao SAR government has been operating smoothly, and civil servants at all levels have exercised their assigned duties, with an unprecedented degree of democratization and openness.

As an unprecedented great practice, the cause of "one country, two systems" still needs to be further explored and advanced; however, we are always full of confidence in the future. "No matter what difficulties or challenges we may encounter, they can never shake our confidence and resolve to uphold the principle and advance the practice of 'one country, two systems'." This is the strongest voice of the times.

2001年5月14日,澳门特别行政区第二届立法会选举投票确定在9月23日举行。按照《中华人民共和国澳门特别行政区基本法》规定,澳门第二届立法会由27名议员组成,其中直接选举产生10名,间接选举10名,行政长官委任7名。这是澳门特区行政暨公职局局长李丽如展示为方便选民而印制的选举手册

On May 14, 2001, it was decided that the election for the 2nd Legislative Council of the Macao SAR would take place on September 23. According to the Basic Law of the Macao Special Administrative Region (MSAR) of the PRC, the composition of the new council with 27 members, would be 10 directly elected, 10 indirectly elected and seven appointed by the Chief Executive. Picture shows Li Liru, director general of the Public Administration and Civil Service Bureau of the Macao SAR, displaying the election handbook printed for voters.

2005年10月29日,第四届东亚运动会在澳门开幕。来自9个国家和地区的近2000名运动员参加17个大项的角逐。这是第四届东亚运动会吉祥物"柏柏"出现在开幕式上

On October 29, 2005, the 4th East Asian Games opened in Macao. Some 2,000 athletes from nine countries and regions were due to take part in 17 major events. Picture shows the games mascot "Pak Pak" at the opening ceremony.

第二章 "一国两制" 澳人治澳
II. One Country, Two Systems, Macao People Governing Macao 033

1 | 2

1, 2. 北京奥运圣火历史性走进澳门大街小巷
Passing the Beijing Olympic torches in the streets of Macao in 2008.

1 | 2

1,2. 2013年6月26日,体操奥运冠军李小鹏(上)在澳门粤华中学表演"李小鹏跳"。当日,由中国澳门体育暨奥林匹克委员会及澳门特区政府体育发展局合办的奥运金牌运动员访问澳门系列活动举行,奥运冠军参观澳门学校,与学生互动。
On June 26, 2013, Olympic gymnastics champion Li Xiaopeng (upper) performed his "Li Xiaopeng Jump" at Yuet Wah College, Macao. On this day, a number of Olympic gold medalists organized by the Olympic Sports and Olympic Committee of Macao and Sports Bureau of Macao SAR Government visited local schools.

036 莲花盛开
BLOOMING LOTUS FLOWER

2013年，澳门大学新校区在珠海横琴落成启用

In 2013, the new campus of the University of Macau opened in Hengqin, Zhuhai.

038 莲花盛开
BLOOMING LOTUS FLOWER

1 | 2

1,2. 2013年，澳门大学位于珠海横琴的新校园启用
The new campus of the University of Macau in Hengqin, Zhuhai was put into use in 2013.

莲花盛开
BLOOMING LOTUS FLOWER

2018年，教育部赠澳大"博雅之壁"，喻弘扬中华优秀传统文化美德

In 2018, the Ministry of Education presented the "Wall of Great Wisdom" to the University of Macau, encouraging it to carry forward the traditional Chinese virtues.

澳大湖景

A shot of the University of Macau.

2019年，澳大毕业典礼
Graduation ceremony of the University of Macau in 2019.

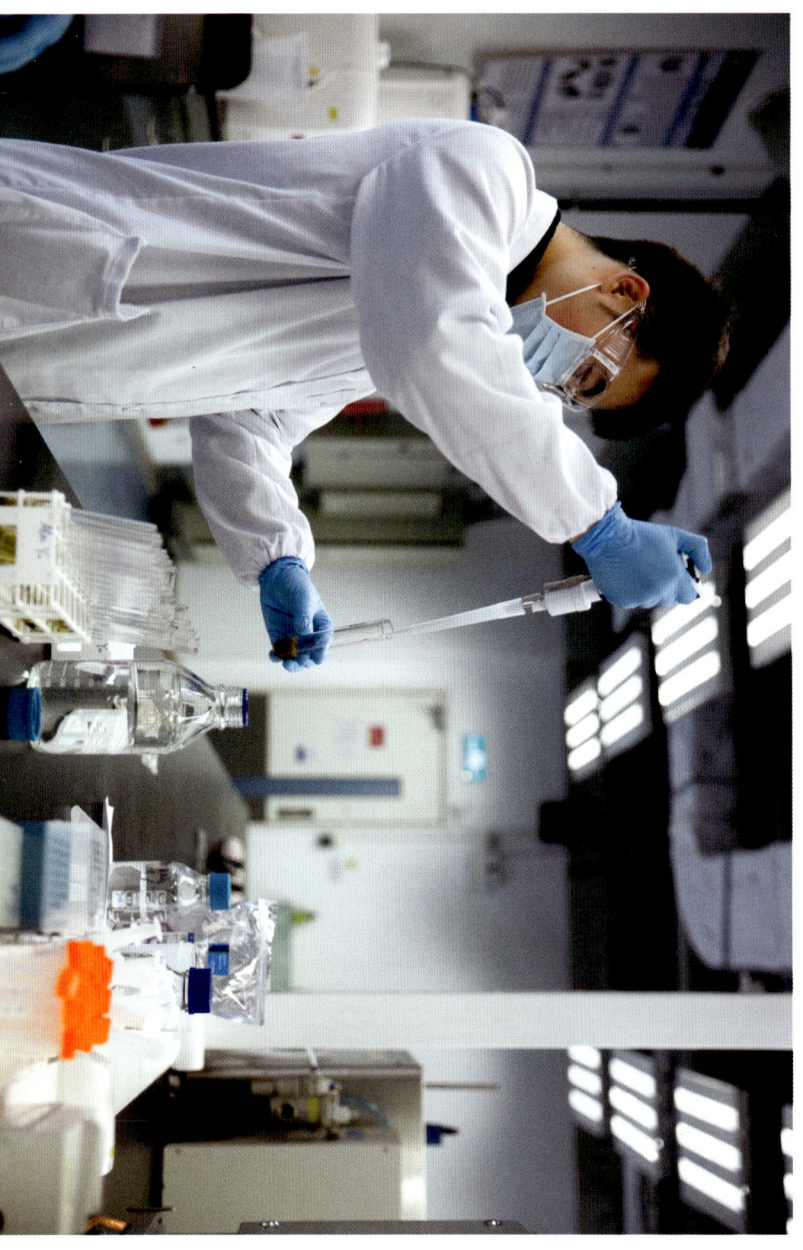

澳大近年的科研有长足发展
The University of Macau has made great progress in scientific research in recent years.

澳大师生正在进行讨论
Discussion between teachers and students at the University of Macau.

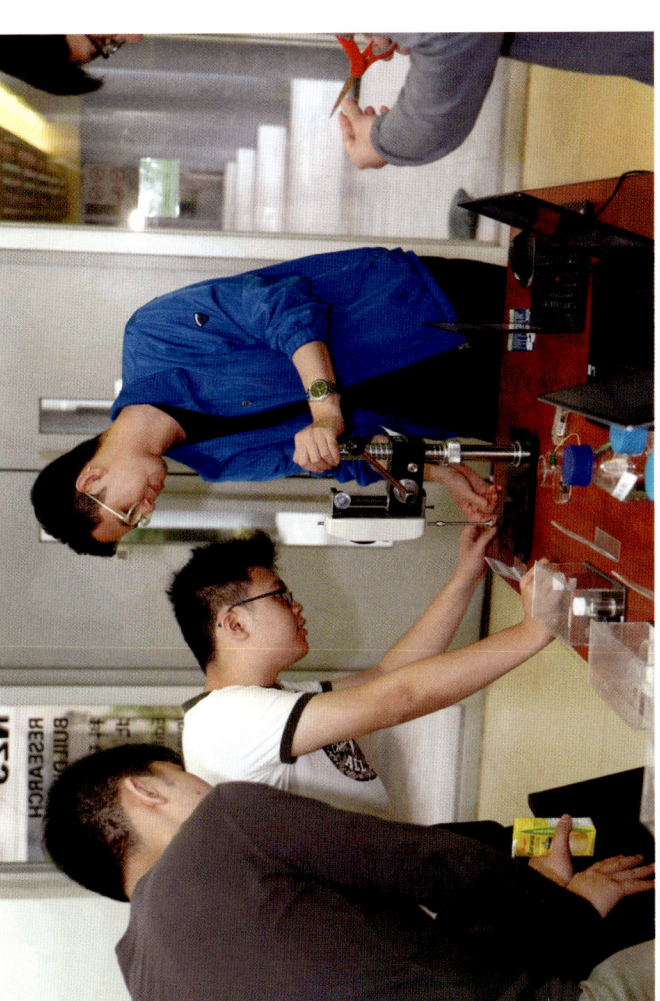

$\dfrac{1\ |\ 2}{3}$

1. 不少中学生到澳大开放日感受大学生活
   A large number of middle school students experience university life at the opening day of the University of Macau.

2. 国际美食节是澳大开放日很受欢迎的活动
   The International Food Festival proves a popular event at the opening day of the University of Macau.

3. 大众借澳大开放日体验实验
   "Experiencing university life" experiment at the opening day of the University of Macau.

习近平主席关于澳门高校工作重要指示精神传达学习会
澳门科技大学
2018年6月16日

澳科大全面贯彻落实习近平主席关于澳门高校工作重要指示精神，旨在培养更多爱国爱澳人才，创造更多科技成果，助力澳门经济适度多元可持续发展及粤港澳大湾区建设

MUST fully implements the gist of the important instruction of President Xi Jinping to cultivate more talents who love the motherland and Macao, seek to produce more scientific and technological achievements and contribute to the sustainable development of a moderately diversified economy of Macao as well as development of the Guangdong-Hong Kong-Macao Greater Bay Area.

伴随特区一起成长的澳门科技大学,发展迅速,已成为澳门规模最大的综合型大学,也是海峡两岸暨港澳五十强大学之一。
Growing with the Macao SAR, MUST has developed rapidly and become the largest comprehensive university in Macao, and being among the top 50 universities in both sides of the Taiwan Straits and Hong Kong and Macao.

046 莲花盛开
BLOOMING LOTUS FLOWER

2018年3月27日，澳科大举行澳门高校首次升国旗仪式，旨在深化学生的爱国爱澳教育，培养学生的国民身份认同及爱国情怀

On March 27, 2018, MUST held the first flag-raising ceremony among the colleges and universities in Macao with a view to deepening education to promote love for the motherland and Macao and cultivating their sense of identity as a citizen and a patriot.

回归20载，澳科大的飞跃进步正是澳门特区高等教育发展所取得骄人成绩的光辉缩影

The great progress made by MUST in the past two decades reflects the glorious achievements made by the Macao SAR in developing higher education.

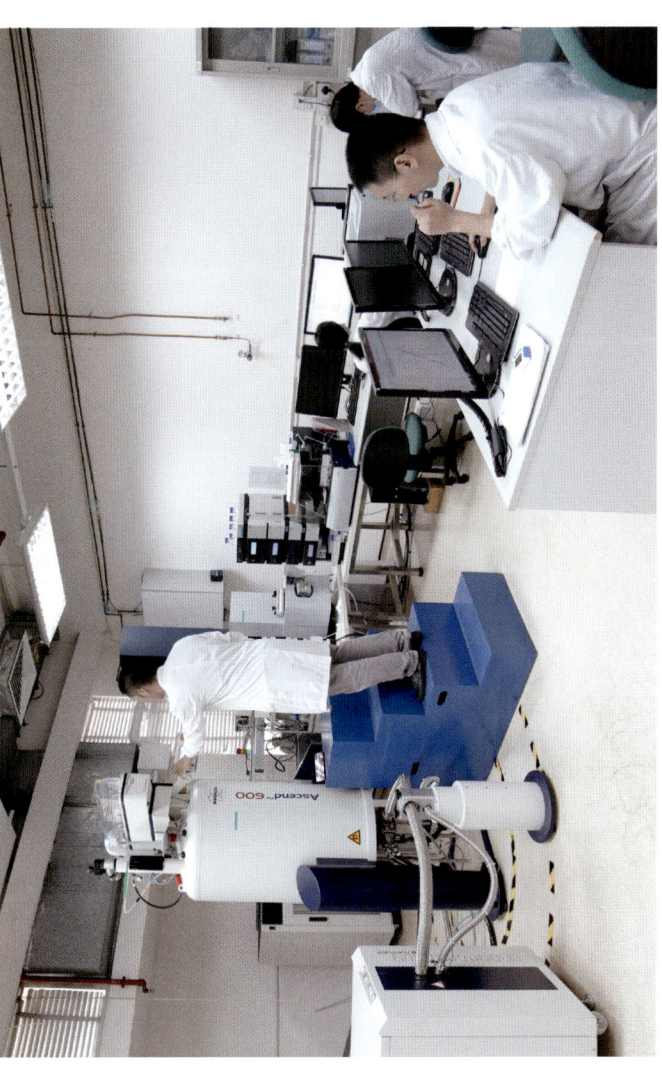
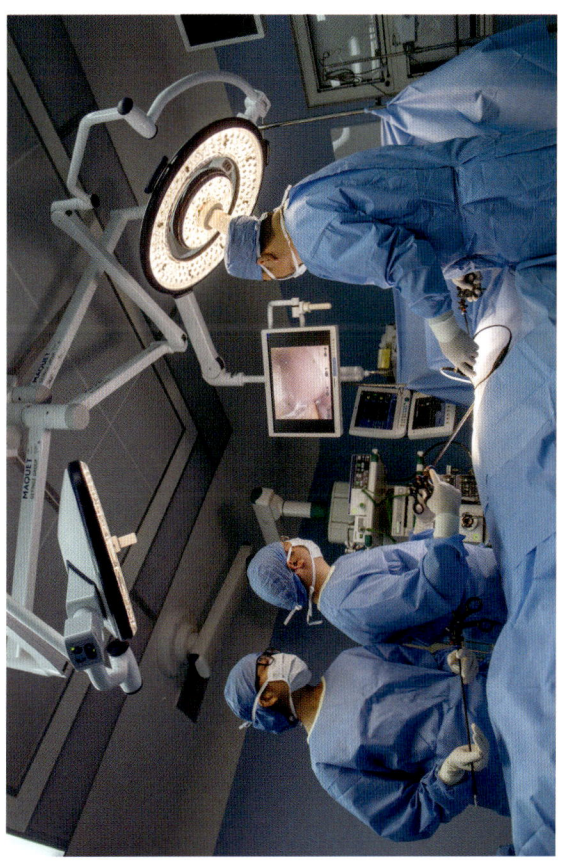
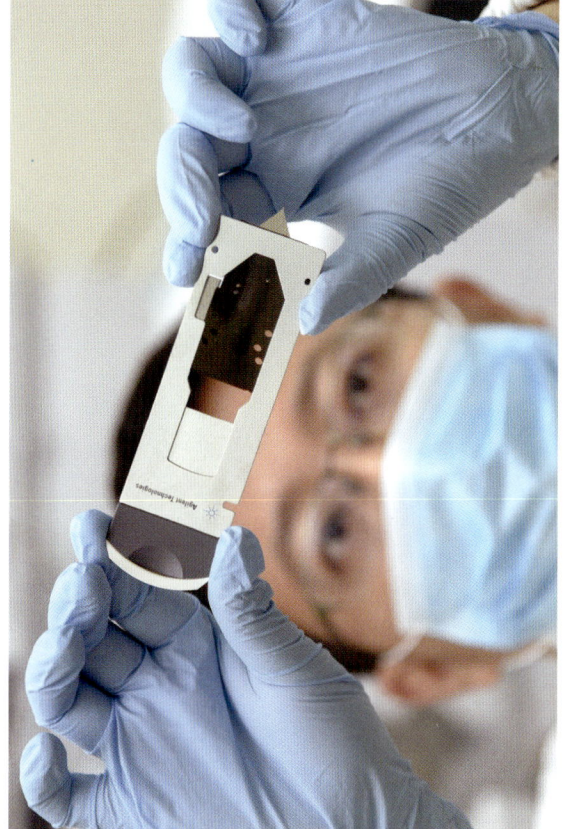

1. 中药质量研究国家重点实验室（澳门科技大学）于2011年1月正式成立，是国家在中医药领域迄今唯一的国家重点实验室

   The State Key Laboratory of Quality Research in Chinese Medicines, under MUST, was formally established in January 2011 as the only one of its kind in China.

2. 澳科大中药质量研究国家重点实验室研究团队成功设计出全球首块TiO2-PGC芯片，其极灵敏的分析技术能够在复杂未知的糖链组成中检测到糖蛋白的痕量糖链的细微变化

   A MUST team successfully designed the world's first TiO2-PGC chip able to detect the slight changes of trace sugar chains of glycoproteins in complex sugar chain composition with extremely sensitive analytical technology.

3. 2019年3月1日，澳门特区首个医学院——澳门科技大学医学院正式成立，开设澳门首个"内外全科医学士学位"课程

   On March 1, 2019, the MUST Faculty of Medicine, the first medical school in the Macao SAR, was formally established, opening an inaugural "Bachelor of Medicine and Bachelor of Surgery" program.

$$\frac{1}{2} \Big| 3$$

1、2. 澳科大月球与行星科学国家重点实验室是中国在天文与行星科学领域首个国家重点实验室,参与嫦娥项目的核心研究

The State Key Laboratory of Lunar and Planetary Sciences in MUST is the first State key laboratory of its kind, participating in core research of the Chinese Lunar Exploration Program.

3. 澳科大月球与行星科学国家重点实验室设有超算中心,助力嫦娥工程的科学数据分析和研究

The State Key Laboratory of Lunar and Planetary Sciences in MUST has a super-calculation center to assist in the scientific data analysis and research for the Chinese Lunar Exploration Program.

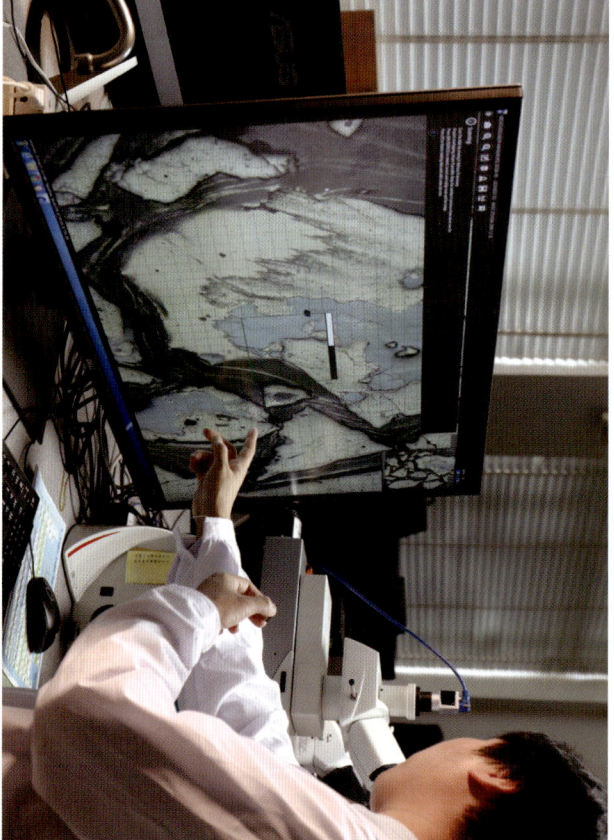
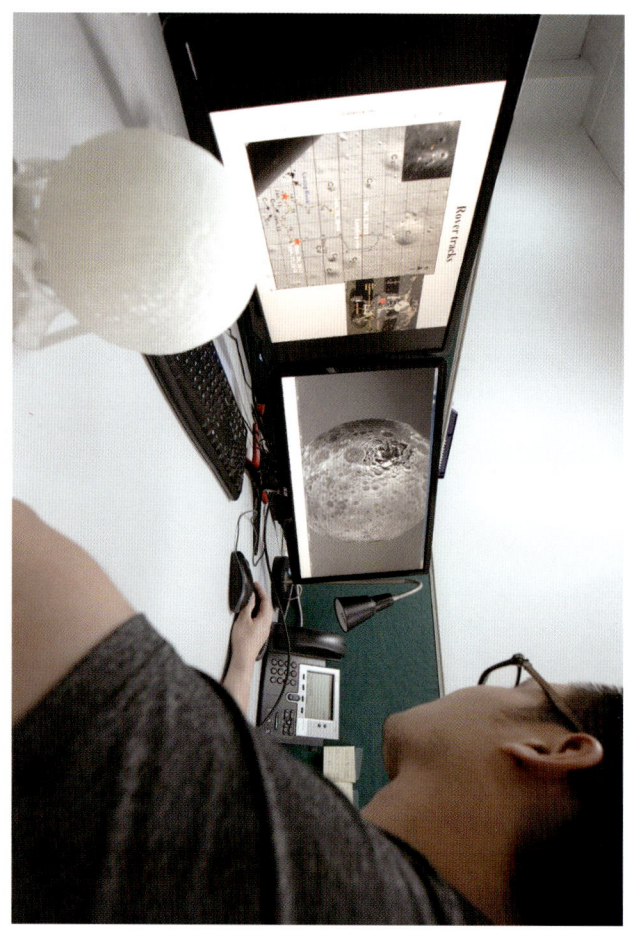

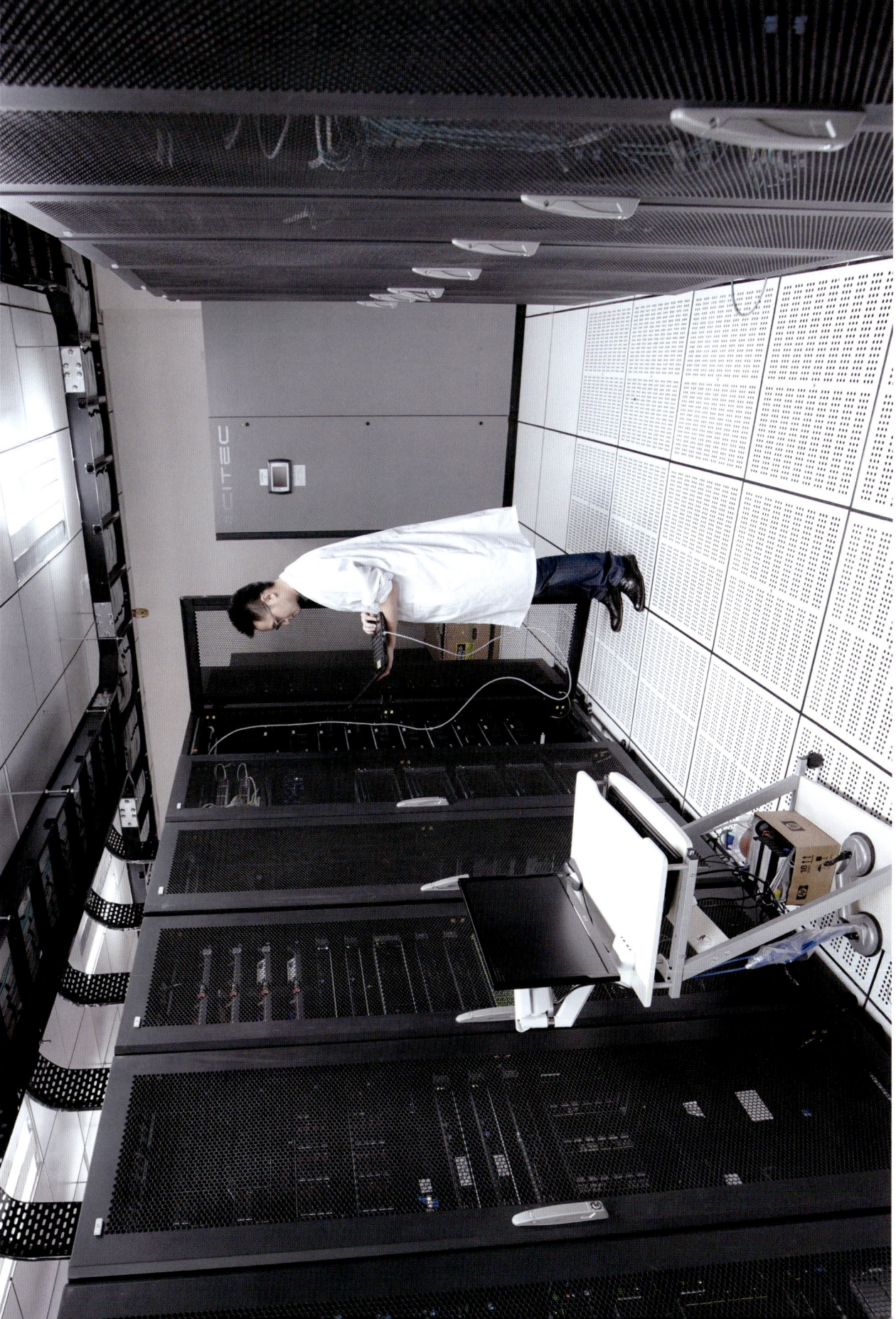

050 莲花盛开
BLOOMING LOTUS FLOWER

2015年，国务院划定澳门85平方公里的水域管理范围和陆地界限

In 2015, the State Council delineated the boundaries of the water and land area of Macao SAR covering 85 square km.

2016年，澳门特区政府发布首个"五年发展规划"
In 2016, the Macao SAR government unveiled its first five-year plan for economic and social development.

2017年6月8日,"一带一路"与澳门发展国际研讨会举行。来自中国、葡萄牙、泰国和巴西等国家的政界人士以及海内外商界、侨界领袖、专家学者等,就"一带一路"发展愿景,以及"一带一路"建设带来的机遇交换意见
On June 8, 2017, the International Conference on Belt and Road and Macao's Development opened in the Macao SAR. Political figures from China, Portugal, Thailand, Brazil and other countries as well as domestic and overseas business leaders, overseas Chinese leaders, experts and scholars, exchanged views on the development vision of the Belt and Road and the opportunities brought about by the expanded Belt and Road.

2018年6月21日,澳门特区行政长官崔世安在珠海横琴参观考察澳门青年创业谷
On June 21, 2018, Chief Executive Chui Sai On visited the Hengqin Entrepreneurship Valley for Macao Youth in neighboring Hengqin, Zhuhai.

054 莲花盛开
BLOOMING LOTUS FLOWER

港珠澳大桥是"一国两制"框架下粤港澳三地首次合作建设的大型跨海交通工程,也是世界上最长的跨海大桥工程。

The Hong Kong-Zhuhai-Macao Bridge is the first large-scale cross-sea traffic project jointly built by Guangdong Province, Hong Kong and Macao SAR under the framework of "one country, two systems." It is the longest cross-sea bridge in the world.

2019年2月21日，由"广东省人民政府、香港特别行政区政府、澳门特别行政区政府共同举办的"粤港澳大湾区发展规划纲要宣讲会"在香港海洋公园万豪酒店举行

Sponsored by the governments of Guangdong Province, Hong Kong SAR and Macao SAR Government, the Symposium on the Outline Development Plan for the Guangdong-Hong Kong-Macao Greater Bay Area was held in Hong Kong Ocean Park Marriott Hotel on February 21, 2019.

2019年3月30日,澳门特区行政长官崔世安出席庆祝澳门回归20周年"千人汇"汇员大会暨与特首面对面活动

On March 30, 2019, Chief Executive Chui Sai On attended the "1,000 Talents" Gathering and "Face-to-Face Meeting with the Chief Executive" in celebration of the 20th anniversary of Macao's return to the motherland.

第三章

善抓机遇 经济飞跃

依托内地，小舞台上演大戏码

III.

Achieving Leapfrog Economic Development by Seizing the Opportunities in a Timely Way

Depending on the Hinterland to Put on a Big Play on a Small Stage

第三章 善抓机遇 经济飞跃
III. Achieving Leapfrog Economic Development by Seizing the Opportunities in a Timely Way

俗话说："某子上唱大戏——摆布不开。"澳门是典型的微型经济体，自身经济资源发展空间有限。但由于背靠祖国内地的广阔市场，回归20年来，澳门在"小舞台上演大戏码"，经济实现了跨越式发展。20年的实践证明，"只要路子对，政策灵，身段灵，人心齐，某子上也可以唱大戏"。

优先解决经济发展问题，是澳门特区政府一直以来的施政重点。在中央政府和祖国内地、特区政府和澳门同胞的共同努力下，回归后，澳门经济发展方面赢得"好评如潮"。可以说，"一国两制"在澳门的逐步成型、成熟，正是建立在澳门经济快速发展和全面繁荣发展的基础之上。

回归前，澳门经济曾连续4年出现负增长，投资者望而却步。回归后，澳门特区政府本着"固本培元，稳健发展"的施政理念，扎扎实实推进经济重建，经济发展逐步走出困局，开始快速复苏。

自2001年起，澳门一直保持年均双位数的高增长态势。2000年，澳门GDP为539亿澳门元，人均1.6万美元；到了2018年，澳门GDP已升至4403亿澳门元，人均GDP是全世界最高的地区之一。

博彩业和旅游业的复苏和振兴是澳门经济形势全面回暖的最著显的最显著标志。2002年，澳门赌权开放，外资博彩企业进入，澳门的博彩业不仅没有受到限制，反而变得更加规范化、现代化和国际化，其成功经验不断被其他国家和地区借鉴学习。同时，旅游业也重新焕发活力，澳门入境游客总数从1999年的744万人次增长至2018年的3600万人次，相当于每天至少有10万人在澳门观光旅游；服务业、会展业等也得到了显著发展，来此休闲、购物、洽商的国际游客越来越多，濠江小城呈现出前所未有的繁荣景象。

澳门的经济腾飞，离不开国家不断为其创造机遇，也离不开澳门自身不断开拓创新。面对亚洲金融风暴、非典肆虐及全球性金融危机的挑战，澳门抓住机遇加入WTO，《内地与澳门关于建立更紧密经贸关系的安排》(CEPA)签署，《泛珠三角区域合作框架协议》签署，内地开放澳门"个人游"，国家从"十一五"起将澳门纳入国家整体发展战略等机遇，走出了一条继续保持作为祖国内地对外开放的"窗口""桥梁""国际通道"及"世界旅游休闲中心""国际化的区域性经济贸易服务平台""中国与葡语系国家联通纽带"的经济建设新路。

如今，澳门的目标是实现经济适度多元发展，中央也对此做出了一系列决策部署。支持澳门融入国家发展大局，进行粤港澳大湾区建设，深化泛珠三角区域合作及与内地各地的互利合作，培育会议展览、中医药、特色金融、文化创意等新兴产业，推进世界旅游休闲中心建设，中国和葡语系国家商贸服务平台的建设，深度参与"一带一路"建设……这些决策部署为实现澳门经济适度多元化指明了方向，创造了必要的条件。

20年来，澳门的发展让华夏儿女复感自豪。她所取得的巨大进步和成就，始终与祖国内地的发展紧密联系在一起。今天的澳门，已不再是那个默默无闻的小城，它和世界的距离从未如此之近，它在区域中的角色也从未如此重要。"任重而道远者，不择地而息。"国家改革开放的大门开放得越大，澳门同胞顺时而为，乘势而上，必将在融入国家发展大局中实现更好的发展，共同谱写中华民族伟大复兴的时代篇章。

1991年，中国银行澳门分行大厦于现址落成，成为当时澳门最高的大厦

The Bank of China, Macao Branch completed in 1991, when it was the highest building in Macao.

A common saying has it that "Putting on a big play on a table – too narrow to move." Macao features a typical micro-economy, with limited economic resources and development space. However, depending on the vast market of the hinterland, it has been able to put on a big play on its small stage over the past two decades. Practice has proven that, as long as Macao finds the right way, adopts appropriate policies, takes flexible measures and its people work with one mind, it can also put on a big play on its narrow "stage".

Giving priority to solving the problems of economic development has been the focus in the administration of the Macao SAR government. Thanks to the joint efforts of the Central Government and the hinterland, the SAR government and the Macao compatriots, Macao has won lavish praise for its economic development after its return. It can be said that the principle of "one country, two systems" gradually took shape and matured in Macao, based wholly on rapid economic development and resultant overall prosperity.

Before its return, Macao featured a lack of economic resources, weak foundations, a single-industry structure, high unemployment rate, deteriorating business environment and poor public security. Its economic growth was a negative discouraging investors. After its return, following the concept of "consolidating the foundations and ensuring steady development", the Macao SAR government promoted economic reconstruction in a solid way, gradually escaping from its old predicament in economic development. As a result, its economy began to recover quickly.

Since 2001, Macao has maintained double-digit average annual growth. In 2000, its GDP was 53.9 billion Pataca de Macau, averaging US$16,000 per capita. In 2018, Macao's GDP rose to 440.3 billion Pataca de Macau, and its per-capita GDP is one of the highest.

The recovery and revitalization of the gaming and tourism sectors was the most significant sign of overall economic recovery. In 2002, the gaming rights of Macao were opened, allowing foreign-owned gaming enterprises to enter and seek business opportunities. As a result, the gaming became more standardized, modernized and internationalized. Its successful experience was continuously studied by other countries and regions for their own development. At the same time, the tourism industry also regained its vitality. The total number of tourists to Macao increased from 7.44 million in 1999 to 36 million in 2018, meaning that at least 100,000 people go sightseeing in Macao on average every day.

36 million in 2018, meaning that at least 100,000 people go sightseeing in Macao on average every day. Remarkable progress was made in the services, conference and exhibition sectors. More and more international tourists are arriving for leisure activities, shopping and negotiations. The small city on the banks of the Haojiang River has assumed an unprecedentedly prosperous look.

Macao's economic take-off was attributed to the motherland's assistance in creating opportunities, and its own unceasing efforts in exploration and innovation. Facing the challenges of the Asian financial crisis, the SARS epidemic and the global financial crisis, Macao seized the strategic opportunities of China's accession to the WTO, the signing of the hinterland-Macao Closer Economic Partnership Arrangement (CEPA) and the Pan-Pearl River Delta Regional Cooperation Framework Agreement, the opening of "individual tours" of the hinterland tourists and the hinterland's inclusion of Macao into its overall development since the 11th Five-Year Plan (2006-10), blazing a new trail for economic development. It remains a window, bridge and international channel for the mainland's opening up, as well as a world tourism and leisure center, internationalized regional economic and trade service platform and a link between China and Portuguese-speaking countries.

Today, Macao's goal is to develop a moderately diversified economy, and the Central Government has also made a series of decisions and arrangements to assist in meeting the target. Macao is firmly incorporated into overall national development plans, and strong support is being given to the construction of the Guangdong-Hong Kong-Macao Greater Bay Area, along with deepened cooperation in the Pan-Pearl River Delta region and mutually beneficial cooperation with the rest of the country. There is a strong drive to foster emerging industries such as conferences and exhibitions, Chinese medicine, featured finance and cultural creativity, promote the building of a world tourism and leisure center and a service platform for trade between China and Portuguese-speaking countries, and deeply participate in the Belt and Road Initiative. These decisions clearly guide the direction and create the necessary conditions for Macao to develop a moderately diversified economy.

Every Chinese takes pride in Macao's development over the past two decades. The tremendous progress and achievements made are always closely linked to the development of the hinterland. Today's Macao is no longer an unknown small and sleepy city. It has never been so close to the world, and its role in the region has never been so important. "Those who shoulder heavy tasks and have a long way to go will never stop to rest anywhere" is an applicable old saying in this regard. As China is opening wider to the outside world, Macao compatriots follow the trend and take advantage of the situation. Macao will surely achieve better development after integrating into the overall development of China and contribute its share to the great rejuvenation of the Chinese nation.

澳门立法会在 2001 年通过《娱乐场幸运博彩经营法律制度》（俗称"博彩法"）
The Legal System of Lucky Gambling Operation in the Casino (commonly known as the "Gambling Law") adopted by the Legislative Assembly of Macao in 2001.

2003年10月11日，澳门旅游塔会展娱乐中心张贴着"中国—葡语国家经贸合作论坛"的宣传海报。首届中国—葡语国家经贸合作论坛于10月12日至14日在这里举行，中国及7个葡语国家主管经贸的部长率领官员率领代表团出席了论坛的多项活动

Poster announcing the Forum for Economic and Trade Cooperation between China and Portuguese-speaking Countries held at the Macao Tower Convention & Entertainment Center. The event was held from October 12 to 14, 2003. Ministers in charge of economy and trade in China and seven Portuguese-speaking countries attended.

亚洲最大综合旅游度假村威尼斯人于2007年开业
Macao delegation went to Shanghai in 2018 to attend the third session of the First China International Import Exposition

2014年9月13日,第八届亚太经合组织(APEC)旅游部长会议在澳门召开

The 8th APEC Tourism Ministerial Meeting held in Macao on September 13, 2014.

070 莲花盛开
BLOOMING LOTUS FLOWER

2017年澳门服装节，以服装为桥梁，让设计师和时装品牌与来自世界各地的参展商进行经贸交流。
The 2017 Macao Fashion Festival for exchanges between designers and fashion brands and exhibitors from all over the world to promote trade.

2018年7月10日,惠澳两地青年交流会
Exchange Meeting between the youth of Huizhou and Macao on July 10, 2018.

莲花盛开
BLOOMING LOTUS FLOWER

联合国教科文组织将澳门评选为"创意城市美食之都",为澳门带来更多发展机会,不单可借此推广本地独特的美食文化,更可促进旅游业的可持续发展,推动澳门朝着建设世界旅游休闲中心的目标迈进。

UNESCO selected Macao as a "Creative City of Gastronomy", bringing it more development opportunities to promote its unique food culture and sustainable development of tourism. Macao seeks to be a world center of tourism and leisure.

在贯彻弘扬中华文化和保留澳门多元文化特色的方针政策下,特区政府举办不同表现形式的文化艺术活动,邀请澳门以及来自内地和世界各地的艺术团体在澳演出,让观众有机会了解不同地方的历史、社会和文化艺术,促进文化交流。

Under the guidelines of carrying forward the Chinese culture and preserving the multicultural characteristics of Macao, the SAR government organizes cultural and artistic activities in different forms, and invites local art groups and those from the hinterland and other places around the world to perform in Macao so that the audiences can learn about the history, society, culture and art of different places. The aim is to promote cultural exchanges.

$\dfrac{2}{3}$

1、2、3. 澳门代表团于 2018 年 11 月赴上海参加首届中国国际进口博览会

The Macao delegation attended the 1st China International Import Expo in Shanghai in November 2018.

莲花盛开
BLOOMING LOTUS FLOWER

经过近30年的发展和完善，澳门的金融体系已成为区域内具有自身发展特点的现代化开放型的金融体系

After nearly 30 years of development and improvement, Macao's financial system has become a modern and open financial system with its own characteristics.

2017年12月12日晚上，粤港澳大湾区城市旅游联合会在广东珠海正式成立

The Guangdong-Hong Kong-Macao Greater Bay Area City Tourism Union formally established in Zhuhai, Guangdong Province, on December 12, 2017.

中国银行澳门分行

中国银行澳门分行前身为"澳门南通银行",由爱国商人庄世平先生于1950年6月创立,1987年元旦正式更名为"中国银行澳门分行",成为中行第九家海外分行。

近七十年来,中国银行澳门分行秉承"根植澳门·服务澳门"的经营宗旨,逐步发展成为本地全功能主流银行,主要从事公司金融、个人金融和金融市场业务等商业银行服务。分行肩负着特区澳门币发钞代理行,政府公库代理行,银行公会主席行,银行同业港元/美元票据清算行及人民币清算行的职责;并通过一系列金融创新,推动特色金融发展,助力特区政府发挥澳门所长,服务国家所需。

近年来,分行积极拓展投行类业务,结构化融资业务,综合性跨境金融服务,为客户提供更多的国际化专业服务,满足客户多元化金融需求。同时,分行还积极配合特区政府农法施政,大力推动特色金融发展和智慧城市建设。

Bank of China Macau Branch

Established by the patriotic businessman Mr. Zhuang Shiping in June 1950 and formerly known as "Nam Tung Bank" in Macao, formally renamed as Bank of China Macau Branch on the New Year's Day in 1987, and became the 9th overseas branch of Bank of China.

In the past 70 years, Bank of China Macau Branch has upheld the principle of "Rooted in Macao, Steadfast in Serving" for nearly seventy years and has become a mainstream and first-choice bank in Macao. Bank of China Macau Branch provides corporation banking, personal banking and related financial services. Acting as one of the two note-issuing banks and the agent bank for the Public Treasury, we are also the Chairman of the Macau Association of Banks and the Clearing Bank for Hong Kong Dollar, US Dollar and RMB. Through a series of financial innovation, promote the development of characteristic finance, help the Macao SAR government to show the advantages of Macao and serve the country.

In recent years, Bank of China Macau Branch actively expands business in investment banking, structural financing, and comprehensive cross-border banking services in order to provide better internationalized professional services for customers and meet their various financial needs. At the same time, we are giving full support to the Macao SAR government's administration and the development of characteristic finance and the construction of smart cities.

1951 年，南通银行成立一周年时全体同事同事留影
A group photo of the staff of the Nantong Bank celebrating its 1st anniversary in 1951.

1987年，南通银行正名为"中国银行澳门分行"。
Nantong Bank was officially renamed as the Bank of China Macau Branch in 1987.

2011年,澳门特区政府向中国银行澳门分行颁授了"工商功绩勋章"。中国银行是首家获此殊荣与美誉的商业机构

The Bank of China Macau Branch was awarded the "Industrial & Commercial Merit Medal" by the Macao SAR government in 2011, becoming the first business organization to gain this honor.

2019年,中国银行澳门分行首只澳门特色大湾区公募基金成立

The first Macao-based Greater Bay Area Public Fund was established by the Bank of China Macau Branch in 2019.

第三章 善抓机遇 经济飞跃
III. Achieving Leapfrog Economic Development by Seizing the Opportunities in a Timely Way

2019年4月2日,《粤港澳大湾区发展规划纲要》澳门首份银政合作协议签署

The first agreement on cooperation between the banking sector and the government of Macao under the Outline Development Plan for the Guangdong-Hong Kong-Macao Greater Bay Area was signed on April 2, 2019.

1949年10月，何耀光院长在镜湖医院庆祝新中国成立大会上发表重要讲话

Kiang Wu Hospital Director Ke Lin made an important speech at the meeting in celebration of the founding of the PRC in October 1949.

1978年9月5日，柯麟院长与镜湖医院员工见面
Kiang Wu Hospital Director Ke Lin met with staff members on September 5, 1978.

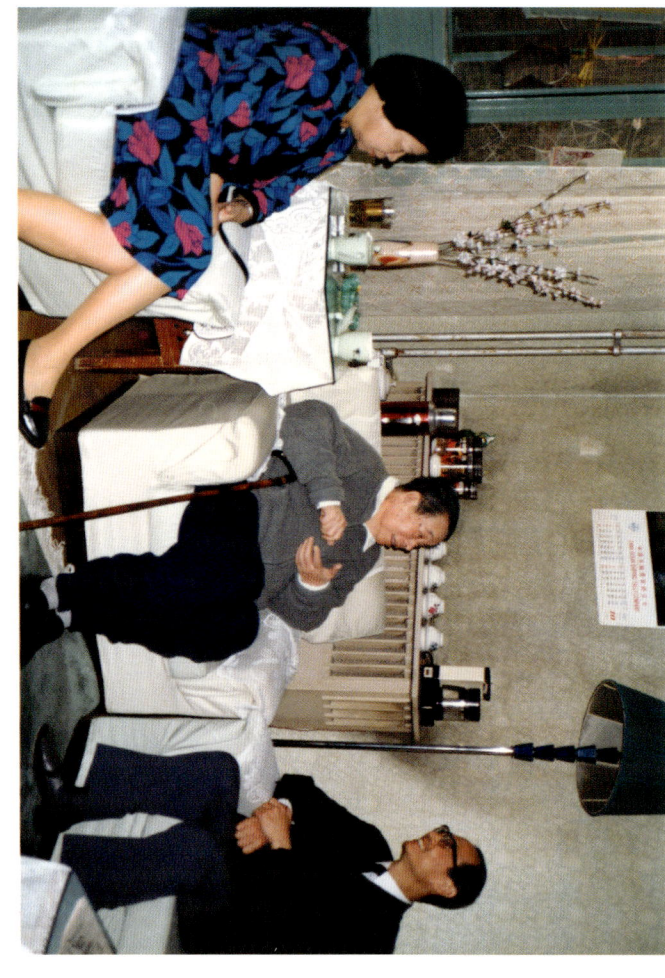

1989年，何鑭名誉主席与卫生部陈敏章部长及镜湖慈善会秘书长梁秀珍合影

A group photo containing Honorary Chairman Ke Lin, Minister of Health Chen Minzhang and Secretary General of the Kiang Wu Charitable Association Liang Xiuzhen in 1989.

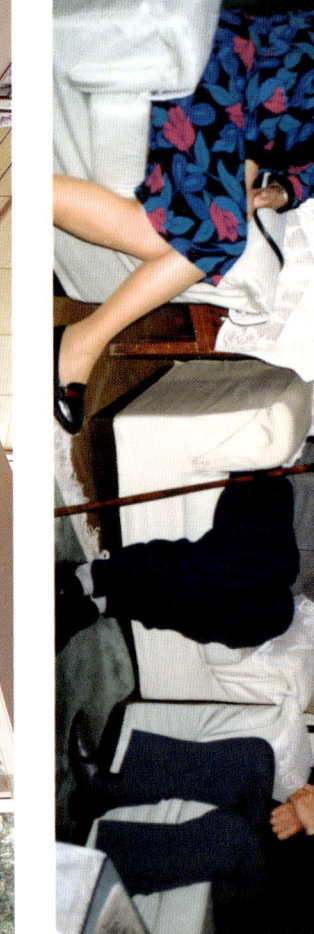

2000年9月10日，卫生部部长张文康莅临镜湖医院

Minister of Health Zhang Wenkang visited Kiang Wu Hospital on September 10, 2000.

2005年6月5日，卫生部高强部长莅临镜湖慈善会和镜湖医院视察
Minister of Health Gao Qiang inspected Kiang Wu Charitable Assocation and Kiang Wu Hospital on June 5, 2005.

2002年6月,廖泽云副主席、吴培娟秘书长率团访问台湾中山医学大学附设医院,签订两院《建立友好合作关系协议书》

In June 2002, Vice Chairman Liao Zeyun and Secretary General Wu Peijuan led a delegation to visit the hospital affiliated to Chung Shan Medical University in Taiwan, and sign an Agreement on the Establishment of a Friendly Partnership between the two hospitals.

2010年6月14日,中山大学、镜湖医院"临床教学协议签署暨中山大学教学医院挂牌仪式"在澳门举行

The Clinical Teaching Agreement Signing Ceremony & Opening Ceremony of the Teaching Hospital of Sun Yat-Sen University held by it and Kiang Wu Hospital in Macao on June 14, 2010.

2011年7月1日,中山大学附属第一医院与镜湖医院友好合作协议书续约仪式

A Signing ceremony for renewal of the Cooperative Agreement between the First Affiliated Hospital of Sun Yat-Sen University and Kiang Wu Hospital held on July 1, 2011.

2015年11月5日，广州中山大学校长罗俊一行9人访问镜湖

A delegation of nine members led by Luo Jun, President of Sun Yat-Sen University in Guangzhou, visited Kiang Wu on November 5, 2015.

2018年10月8日，粤港澳大湾区三机构签署医疗合作协议

A medical cooperation agreement signed by three institutions in the Guangdong-Hong Kong-Macao Greater Bay Area signed on October 8, 2018.

2018年8月,"银娱澳门杯——第10届青少年国情知识竞赛"访京团一行参观被命名为"吕志和楼"的北京大学新生命科学科研楼。
A delegation attending the "GEG Macao Cup – 10th Youth National Condition Knowledge Contest" visited the new life science research building of Peking University named "Lui Che Woo Building" in August 2018.

2018年8月31日，第7届"银娱青少年成就计划"获奖学员参观泰中罗勇工业园，了解"一带一路"框架下中泰产业合作概况

Award-winning students of the 7th GEG Youth Achievement Program visited the Thai-Chinese Rayong Industrial Zone in eastern Thailand to learn about industrial cooperation under the Belt and Road Initiative on August 31, 2018.

2018年12月19日，银娱为员工安排多场《港珠澳大桥》纪录片专场

Galaxy Entertainment Group screened a documentary entitled Hong Kong-Zhuhai-Macao Bridge for employees repeatedly in December 2018.

银娱安排中国金牌运动员到澳大吕志和书院与学生交流,致力为澳门青少年搭建开拓视野的平台
Galaxy Entertainment Group invited Chinese medalists to the Lui Che Woo Colledge at the University of Macau to exchange views with the students there, as part of its commitment to building a platform for Macao youth to widen their vision.

2019年1月,银娱举办"金猪贺岁——银娱爱心千岁宴"新春联欢活动,与近百名长者于"澳门百老汇"欢乐地提前欢度新春
GEG held a celebratory Spring Festival carnival with some 100 elders at the Broadway Macao in January, 2019.

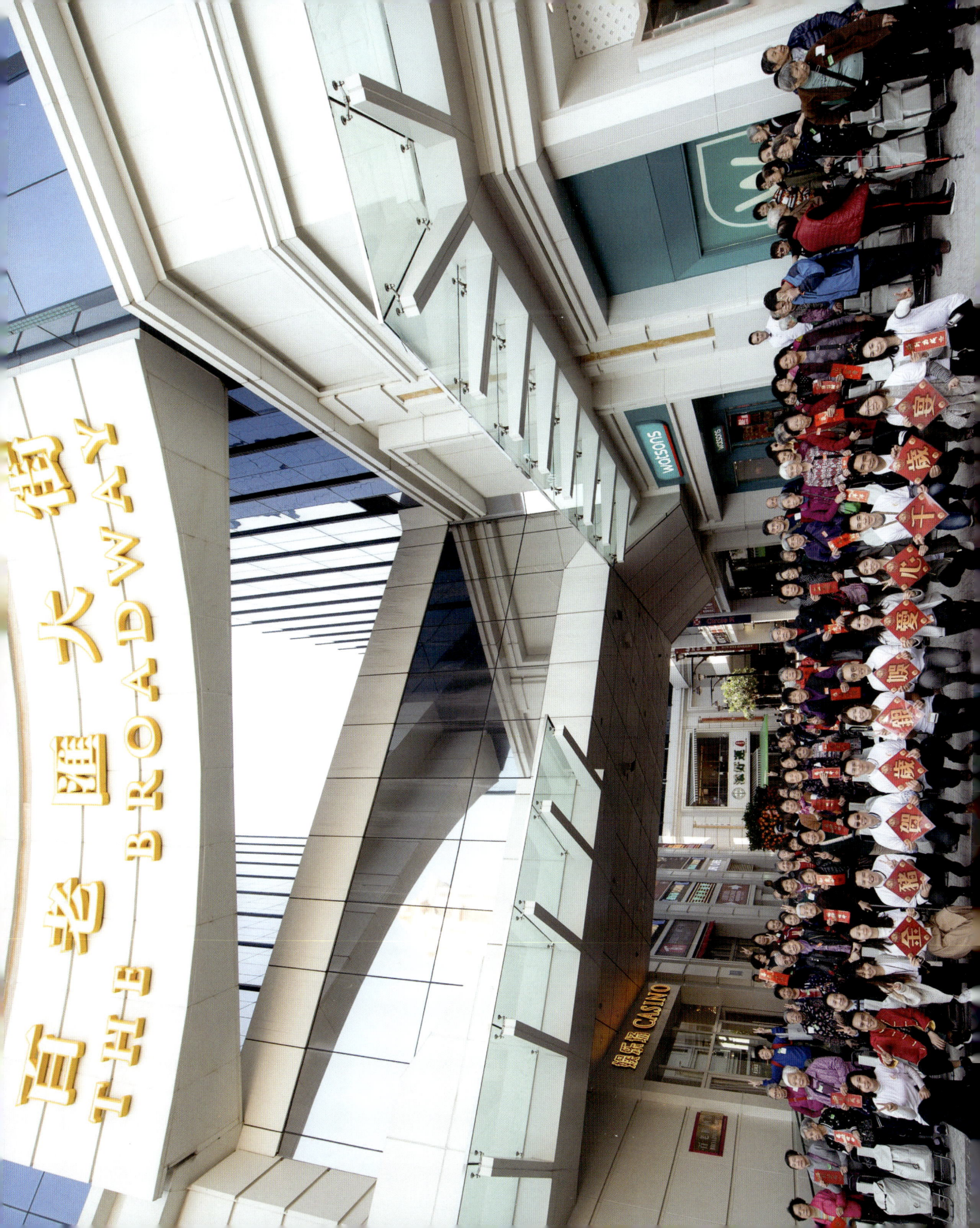

1952 年 10 月 1 日，庆祝中华人民共和国成立 3 周年，南光公司职工在公司天台上合影留念
A group photo of Nam Kwong Company employees taken on the company's roof to mark the 3rd anniversary of the founding of the PRC.

1961 年 6 月，澳门中国旅行社成立
China Travel Service (Macao) opened in June 1961.

第三章 善抓机遇 经济飞跃
III. Achieving Leapfrog Economic Development by Seizing the Opportunities in a Timely Way

1999年12月20日,南光集团组织员工热烈欢迎中国人民解放军驻澳部队进驻澳门
On December 20, 1999, the Nam Kwong Group organized employees to warmly welcome the Chinese PLA Macao Garrison.

自2004年以来,南光集团持续在澳门高校设立"南光教育奖学金",支持澳门教育事业发展,履行企业社会责任
Since 2004, Nam Kwong Group has successively established a "Nam Kwong Education Scholarship" at Macao colleges and universities to support local educational development and fulfill its corporate social responsibilities.

098 莲花盛开
BLOOMING LOTUS FLOWER

2017年8月23日,"天鸽"台风吹袭澳门,南光集团组织义工队清理街道垃圾
On August, 23, 2017, Typhoon Hato hit Macao, Nam Kwong Group organized a volunteer team to clear away rubbish on the streets.

2018年12月9日,南光集团领导参加公益金百万行活动
On December, 9, 2018, leaders of the Nam Kwong Group took part in a Public Welfare Fund Walks for Millions.

2018年12月12日，中华（澳门）金融资产交易股份有限公司揭牌
On December 12, 2018, the Chongwa (Macao) Financial Asset Exchange Co., Ltd. was formally established.

南光集团确保澳门国际机场班机的燃油供应——澳门国际机场班机正在加油
Nam Kwong Group ensures fuel supply for flights from Macao International Airport.

第四章

中西荟萃　包容共济

幸福和谐，多元文化生机勃发

IV. An Inclusive City with Combined Chinese and Western Styles

A Happy and Harmonious Home Featuring Vital Multi-Culture

102 莲花盛开
BLOOMING LOTUS FLOWER

澳门是一座文化城市，历史和文化就是澳门的财富。几百年来，中西文化的交流与嬗变，赋予澳门独特的文化魅力。

漫步在澳门的大街小巷，原汁原味的中西建筑随处可见。中式建筑质朴含蓄，给人以历史的厚重感；西式建筑绚丽典雅，色彩明快，热情洋溢，风情万种。踏入十月初五街、草堆街、火船头街，仿佛一下子回到中国古代社会，这些街市完美地保存着古色古香的中式建筑，置身于澳门市政厅广场，又仿佛来到南欧小城，四周许多拱形门窗、厚实墙壁的欧式楼房，粉红、杏黄、水绿、乳白、色彩明丽，夺人眼目。阳光下，用从葡萄牙运来的黄蓝色小石子铺就的波浪形图案地面，仿佛地中海波光粼粼的海面，走在上面，惬意浪漫。

几百年的时光流过，中西文化在澳门既对立和谐共生，又相融共生。澳门回归后，"一国两制"方针在各方面得到落实，多元文化被温柔地接纳和荟萃发扬。这里是"马照跑、舞照跳"，原有的世界遗产名录》中那句"你们掳去的是我的肉体，你依然保管着我灵魂中的灵魂。"如今，澳门与祖国内地的灵魂相融交织，澳门人的心随着祖国家民族的脉搏而跳动。

不过，无论霓虹灯如何幻彩夺目，无论斗转星移世事如何变迁，在澳门同胞心中，有一样情怀亘古不变，那就是他们深埋心中的爱国热情。他们常说的一句话是："澳门能有今天，祖国是坚强后盾。"这是澳门同胞自豪的心声。在澳门，每时每刻都可以感受祖国的温暖。60多年来，无论春夏秋冬，风雨酷暑，每天都有数百吨鲜活农产品和数十万吨淡水源源不断地从珠海流向澳门，这样的供应从未中止过。每四年一次，8月底9月初，内地奥运精英代表团来丶洗去征尘，就飞抵澳门，以各种方式同民众亲密互动，分享胜利的喜悦、拼搏的艰辛和成长的心路历程。

2017年，澳门遭受强台风"天鸽"正面袭击，驻澳部队应特区政府请求全面出动，参加灾后重建和恢复秩序工作，军民"鱼水之情"熠熠闪光，许多澳门居民在社交媒体中深情留言："最可爱的人来了！"

当神舟载人航天飞行代表团访澳，当奥运火炬高举在澳门的大街小巷，当新中国喜迎70华诞，澳门居民无不全情投入，焕发出无比的爱国热忱和民族自豪感。这是热情参与，也是分享荣光；这是国家的荣耀，更是民族的骄傲。

同样的，澳门同胞多次为内地战胜自然灾害慷慨解囊，同胞之间血浓于水，情同手足。内地人民不会忘记，西藏第一所希望工程小学是澳门同胞捐建的；1998年长江、松花江、嫩江流域发生历史罕见的大水灾，当时40多万人口的澳门向灾区捐款捐物总值达3000多万元；2008年四川汶川大地震，澳门同胞感同身受，捐款总额高达55亿澳门元……每一次扶贫救灾活动，都生动展现着澳门同胞对祖国一往情深的骨肉亲情，他们的行动体现了中华民族的凝聚力。

还记得《七子之歌》中那句"他们掳去的是我的肉体，你依然保管着我灵魂中的灵魂。"如今，澳门与祖国内地的灵魂相融交织，澳门人的心随着祖国家民族的脉搏而跳动。

20年来，在中央政府的支持和帮助下，澳门社会民生福祉得到极大改善，2007年开始全面实施15年免费教育，2008年开始每年开展现金分享计划，2014年填海造地修建公共房屋……居者有其屋，病者有其医，老者有其养，少者有其学，其乐融融，幸福和谐。在这里，积德行善，助人为乐，施比受更有福的理念深入人心，公益慈善义举一呼百应。这些真挚而朴素，包容共济的情怀，凝聚成强大的社会力量，成为澳门繁荣进步的内在源泉和动力。

Macao is a cultural city, with a wealth of history and culture on offer. For centuries, the exchange and transformation of Chinese and Western cultures have resulted in the unique cultural charm of Macao.

Authentic Chinese and Western-style buildings can be seen in the streets of Macao. The plain and subtle Chinese buildings have strong historical features while the gorgeous and elegant Western-style buildings in brisk colors look warm and charming. When walking along the Rua de Cinco de Outubro, Rua Das Estalagens and Rua das Lorchas, one can become submerged in the ancient society of China due to the careful preservation of many old Chinese buildings. Senado Square givers visitors the impression they have been transported to a town in Southern Europe since there are many arched doors and windows, thick square pillars and European-style buildings with thick walls. Their pink, apricot yellow, light green and milky white colors form a gorgeous pattern. In the sunlight, the ground paved with yellow and blue pebbles to form wave pattern looks like the rippling surface of the Mediterranean, providing a romantic feel for those who walk on them.

Hundreds of years have seen harmonious co-existence and blend of Chinese and Western cultures. After Macao's return, the principle of "one country, two systems" was implemented in various aspects, and the multicultural concept was gently accepted and carried forward. All the recreational activities such as horse races and dances continued as before. The Lisboa Casino and other gaming venues are still crowded. A total of 25 historical buildings are included into the World Heritage List. The original art festival, music festival, international dragon boat race and Grand Prix racing continue to flourish.

However, no matter how the place has changed, Macao compatriots have always cherished great patriotic enthusiasm. They often attribute Macao's achievements to the strong support of the motherland, and they are proud of it.

The warmth of the motherland can be felt at all times in Macao. Over the past six decades, hundreds of tons of fresh products and hundreds of thousands of tons of fresh water have been transported from Zhuhai to Macao every day, and such supply has never been interrupted. Once every four years, the Olympic elites of the mainland have always flown to Macao to share their joy of victory.

When Macao was directly hit by Typhoon Hato in 2017, the PLA troops stationed in Macao, at the request of the SAR government, went all out to take part in the post-disaster reconstruction and restoration work. Many Macao residents left a soulful message on social media: "The loveliest people have come!"

During the visit of the Shenzhou manned space flight mission delegation to Macao, the Olympic torch relay across the city, and the celebration for the 70th birthday of the PRC, Macao residents showed their devotion, great patriotic enthusiasm and national pride. This is the glory of the country and also the pride of the nation.

In return, Macao compatriots have repeatedly contributed generously to the natural disaster relief across the hinterland. Hinterland people will never forget the following facts: the first primary school of Project Hope in Tibet was built with the donation

from Macao compatriots: when a historically rare flood occurred in the Yangtze River, Songhua River and Nenjiang River in 1998, the disaster areas received donations worth over RMB 30 million from Macao, which then had a population of some 400,000; and after the Wenchuan earthquake in Sichuan, Macao compatriots made a total donation of 5.5 billion Pataca de Macau... Every poverty alleviation and disaster relief activity offers a vivid expression of the deep love of Macao compatriots for the motherland, and their actions reflect the cohesiveness of the Chinese nation.

We still remember what is said in the *Song of the Seven Songs*: What they have taken away is my flesh and you still have my soul. Today, Macao and the hinterland are of one mind, and share weal and woe.

In the past 20 years, with the support and help of the Central Government, the social welfare cause in Macao has been greatly improved. In 2007, it began to provide 15 years of free education; in the following year, it launched the annual cash sharing program, and in 2014, it undertook land reclamation from the sea to build public housing. Each person has residence, each patient receives medical treatment, each elder is well provided for, and each child is properly educated. All the people live a happy life in a harmonious society. Here, the concept of doing good deeds, helping others, and believing it to be more blessed to give than receive is deeply rooted in the hearts of the people. Macao people are always ready to go into action through public welfare and charitable deeds. These sincere, simple and inclusive feelings have become a powerful source of social power and the internal source and driving force for Macao's prosperity and progress.

澳門格蘭披治大賽車
GRANDE PRÉMIO DE MACAU
MACAU GRAND PRIX

1, 2, 3. 澳門格蘭披治大賽車活動每年11月於澳門舉行
The Macao Grand Prix for both racing cars and motorcycles is held every November.

110 莲花盛开
BLOOMING LOTUS FLOWER

2000年7月,为期一个月的第一届澳门美食节开幕。

In July 2000, the first Macao Food Festival opened for a one-month run.

2005年11月11日，第四届澳门美食节开幕

On November 11, 2005, the fourth Macao Food Festival.

1 | 2

1,2. 澳门历史城区被列入世界遗产名录,成为中国第31处世界遗产
The Historic Centre of Macao is listed as the 31st World Heritage Site in China.

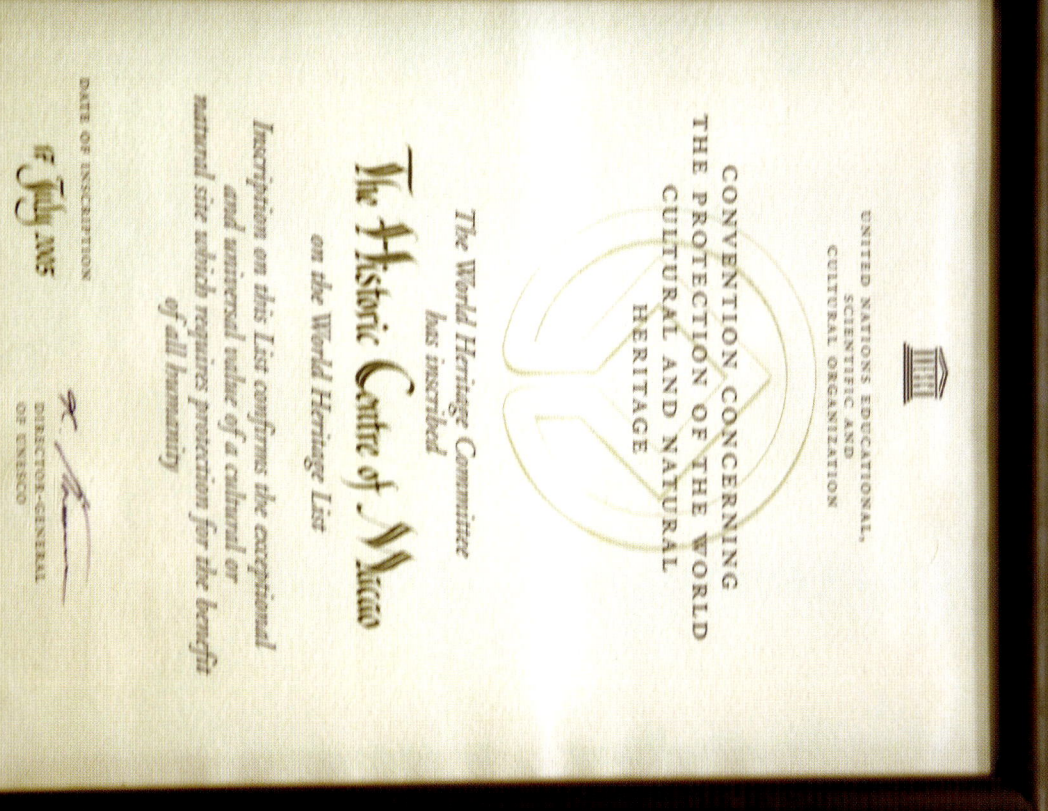

莲花盛开
BLOOMING LOTUS FLOWER

1 | 2
1, 2. 澳门一年一度的国际烟花比赛汇演,澳门的夜空绽放出一幅幅绚丽璀璨的烟花图案
Macao's night sky lit up with an explosion of color during the annual International Fireworks Competition.

2007年10月9日，何鸿燊购宝献国家·圆明园马首铜像展在澳门新葡京酒店拉开帷幕。全国政协常委何鸿燊以6910万港元的价格，购入原属圆明园海晏堂御制12生肖"水力钟"喷泉的马首铜像，并将其捐赠给国家。

On October 9, 2007, an exhibition was held in the Grand Lisboa of Macao to show treasures and the Bronze Horse Head belonging to the 12 zodiac "Water Clock" Fountain of Haiyantang in Beijing's Yuanmingyuan (Old Summer Palace), which Stanley Ho, member of the Standing Committee of the CPPCC National Committee, purchased at Sotheby's Hong Kong for HK$69.1 million and donated to the Central Government.

2007年12月14日，海南农垦供港澳蔬菜首发仪式在三亚市举行，首批满载80吨蔬菜的卡车驶离三亚，运往香港、澳门市场

On December 14, 2007, a ceremony was held at Sanya of Hainan Island to celebrate local vegetables being supplied to Hong Kong and Macao. The first batch of such vegetables, weighing 80 tons, were shipped in trucks to Hong Kong and Macao markets.

2008年6月2日，澳门第二批总计40吨，价值1000万澳门元的赈灾物资，由澳门航空NX9398包机运往四川地震灾区。
On June 2, 2008, Macao's second batch of 40 tons of disaster relief materials valued at 10 million Pataca de Macau was flown by a chartered plane of Air Macau, NX9398, to earthquake-stricken areas in Sichuan Province.

2010年9月9日,澳门地产业总商会向澳门红十字会捐赠20万澳门元,用于援助甘肃舟曲受灾群众

On September 9, 2010, the Macao General Chamber of Commerce for Real Estate Industry donated 200,000 Pataca de Macau to the Macao Red Cross Society for use to assist the victims of the Zhouqu natural disaster in Gansu Province.

1、2、3. 2017年8月24日—28日，驻澳门部队依法协助澳门特区政府救助台风"天鸽"受灾地区

From August 24 to 28, 2017, the PLA Macao Garrison assisted the Macao SAR government in its typhoon rescue work.

驻澳门部队积极举办中国故事文化联谊活动。图为国防知识介绍及互动环节,同学们热情高涨,积极举手回答。

The PLA Macao Garrison actively organized the Chinese Story Culture Fellowship activities. The picture shows the introduction and interaction of national defense knowledge. The students showed their enthusiasm during a lively questions and answers sessions.

驻澳门部队与澳门特区政府教育暨青年局联合举办 "国旗下的说话——澳门中学生国旗手训练营" 活动

The PLA Macao Garrison and the Education and Youth Bureau of the government of the Macao SAR jointly organized a "Speaking under the National Flag" training camp for Macao middle school students.

第四章 中西荟萃 包容共济
IV. An Inclusive City with Combined Chinese and Western Styles

1 | 2

1. 每年的驻澳门部队军营开放日都会吸引万名市民入营参观体验
   Tens of thousands of Macao people visit the PLA Macao Garrison on the annual Camp Open Day.

2. 驻澳门部队军营开放日，澳门市民走进军营体验轻武器操作，增强国防意识
   On the Camp Open Day of the PLA Macao Garrison, Macao citizens enter the barracks to witness operation of light weapons in order to enhance their national defense awareness.

2018年9月16日，超强台风"山竹"来袭，特区政府开放16处避险中心。
On September 16, 2018, Macao was hit by a super typhoon known as Mangosteen. The SAR government opened 16 safe havens for local citizens.

1, 2. 受台风"山竹"影响,澳门迎来降雨和强风,消防员帮助市民疏散

Firefighters helped evacuate residents during the super typhoon Mangosteen.

2008年6月23日，镜湖医院第二批赴四川抗震救灾医疗救护队合影
On June 23, 2008, the second batch of medical rescue teams from Kiang Wu undertake earthquake relief work in Sichuan.

2009年8月17日，澳門鏡湖醫院捐建四川綿陽市永安鎮衛生院暨捐助台灣風災同胞捐款儀式

On August 17, 2009, Kiang Wu Hospital in Macao held a donation ceremony for building Yong an Town Health Center in Mianyang City, Sichuan Province and helping disaster-affected Taiwan compatriots.

2017年8月23日，"天鴿"風災，消防部門緊急提供救命水

August 23, 2017, witnessed the "Sky Pigeon" Wind Disaster Fire Emergency Provision of Life-saving Water delivery event.

2018年2月6日，圣公会（澳门）蔡高中学学生运用由澳区省级政协委员联谊会捐赠的视频设备参与国旗教育活动

On February 6, 2018, students from Chua Senior High School (branch) of Anglican Church (Macao) participate in national flag education activities.

2018年3月19日，氹仔坊众学校（分校）学生使用由澳区省级政协委员联谊会捐赠的视频设备开展国旗教育

On March 19, 2018, students from the Taipa Escola dos Moradores de Macau (branch) viewed educational photos of the national flag.

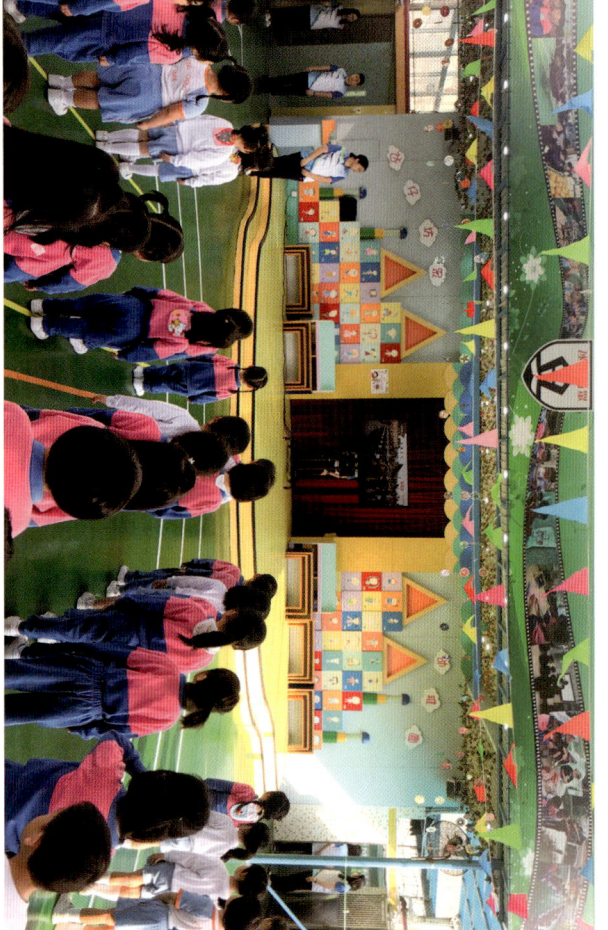

2019年4月17日，在澳区省级政协委员联谊会举办的"政协委员与你分享"活动上，澳门理工学院学生向政协委员提问
On April 17, 2019, Macao Polytechnic Institute students raised questions on topics of concern to CPPCC members.

2019年3月25日，澳门菜农子弟学校学生在由澳区省级政协委员联谊会举办的"政协委员话你知"活动上，与政协委员互动交流
On March 25, 2019, Macao Vegetable Farmers' Children's School students asked questions on topics of concern to a visiting CPPCC member.

1 | 2

1、2. 2019年6月4日，澳区省级政协委员联谊会组织访问团，实地考察贵州省从江县大歹村透风漏雨住房改造项目

On June 4, 2019, Ma Zhiyi, Chairman of the Association of Provincial-level CPPCC Members in Macao, inspects a dilapidated housing renovation project in Dadai Village, Congjiang County.

第四章 中西荟萃 包容共济
IV. An Inclusive City with Combined Chinese and Western Styles

1、2、3. 旅游局自2015年起举办"澳门光影节",于每年12月在澳门半岛及离岛多个景点上演光雕表演等。

Since 2015, the Tourist Bureau has held the Macao Light Festival every December. Light sculptures are set up at various scenic spots on the Macao Peninsula and outlying islands.

136 莲花盛开
BLOOMING LOTUS FLOWER

1 | 2
1,2. 每逢农历新年，澳门各区均会摆放传统灯饰，营造喜气洋洋的过年气氛。
When the Chinese New Year comes in Macao, traditional lighting arrangements create a happy atmosphere.

138 莲花盛开 BLOOMING LOTUS FLOWER

1 | 2 | 3

1, 2, 3. 农历新年期间，澳门举行花车大巡游
During the Chinese New Year, decorated floats are paraded around Macao streets.

第四章 中西荟萃 包容共济
IV. An Inclusive City with Combined Chinese and Western Styles

1 | 2

1, 2. 中秋佳节,澳门各主要街道、广场、圆形地等都布置了节日灯饰,以增添节日气氛

During the Mid-Autumn Festival, the main streets, squares and circular areas of Macao are decorated with festive lights to add festive atmosphere.

142 莲花盛开
BLOOMING LOTUS FLOWER

1 | 2

1, 2. 中秋佳节,澳门国际花灯节
During the Mid-Autumn Festival, the main streets, park squares and circular areas of Macao are decorated with festive lights to add festive atmosphere.

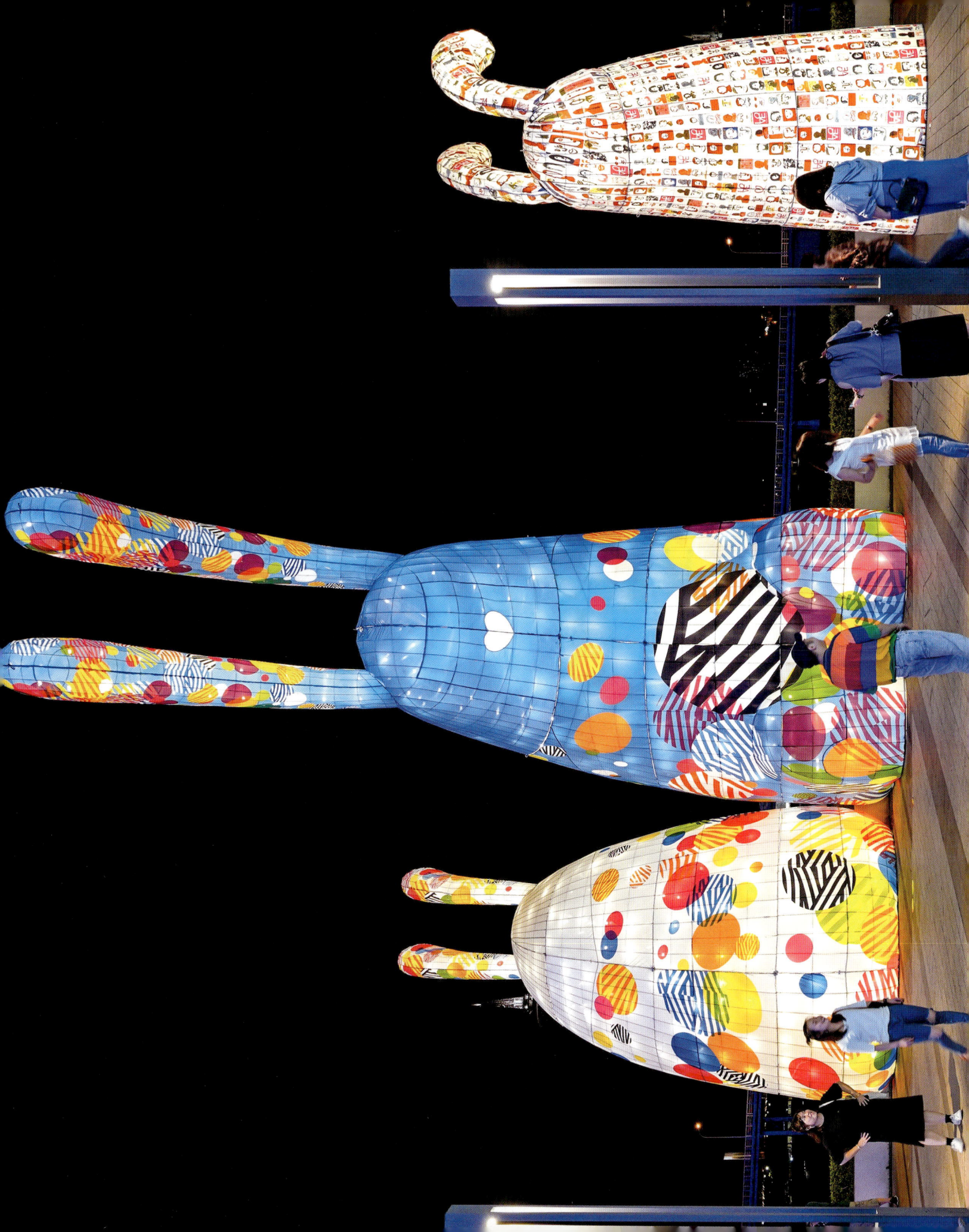

IV. An Inclusive City with Combined Chinese and Western Styles

第四章 中西荟萃 包容共济

145

农历新年期间，澳门举行舞龙活动
During the Chinese New Year, decorated floats are paraded in Macao.

中秋佳节，澳门国际花灯节
During the Mid-Autumn Festival, the main streets, park squares and circular areas of Macao are decorated with festive lights to add festive atmosphere.

1,2. 中央赠送澳门的大熊猫开开和心心从成都机场飞赴澳门，并入住澳门石排湾郊野公园熊猫馆

Macao Giant Pandas presented by the Central Committee flown from Chengdu Airport to Macao happily settle into the Panda Pavilion of the SEAC Pai Van Park of Macao.

中央赠送澳门的大熊猫开开和心心在澳门石排湾郊野公园熊猫馆
Giant Pandas in the Panda Pavilion of the SEAC Pai Van Park of Macao.

第四章 中西荟萃 包容共济
IV. An Inclusive City with Combined Chinese and Western Styles

澳门西湾大桥于 2005 年建成。经历 400 多年的中西文化交融，回归后抓住祖国经济腾飞的机遇，如今的澳门，在传统与现代、东方与西方的交织中流动着独特的色彩

The Sai Wan Bridge in Macao was completed in 2005. After more than 400 years of cultural blending between China and the West, and taking the opportunity of economic development of the motherland after returning to China, Macao now has a unique coloring with the interweaving of tradition and modernity, East and West.

新濠天地和金沙城夜景
City of Dreams and Cotai Central at night.

圣诞夜的民政总署
Civil Affairs Department on Christmas Eve.

华夏国际（澳门）艺术展览中心是一家私人博物馆，创始人创建博物馆的目的是弘扬中华民族文化，为推动澳门文化产业的发展做一点贡献。

Huaxia International (Macao) Art Exhibition Center is a private museum established to promote Chinese culture and contribute to the development of Macao's cultural industry.

1, 2, 3. 馆中文物是包含物质文化和精神文化内涵的器物，也是历史的见证者

Cultural relics in the center containing material and cultural connotations as a witness to Macao's long history.

第五章

凝心聚力　续谱新篇

未来可期，澳门的明天会更好

V.
Making Joint Efforts to Write a New Chapter

Looking forward to a Bright Future

20年前，应着亿万中华儿女的深情呼唤，澳门顺利回归祖国，五星红旗和澳门莲花区旗，迎着海风的吹拂，飘扬在澳门的蓝天白云之下。

20年后，澳门在祖国母亲的怀抱中，享受着关怀和温暖，有一种难以述说的幸福。回归20年，是澳门人对祖国认同感、归属感不断增强的20年，是澳门人"爱国爱澳"情怀高涨的20年。澳门，不再是飘零异乡的游子，而是"中国澳门"！

背靠祖国，面向世界，澳门创造了一个又一个经济奇迹，彰显着"一国两制"方针强大的生命力和巨大的优越性。昔日小小濠镜澳，如今长成大都市。碧海上高高耸立的观光旅游塔，在阳光照耀下冲天而起，饱合活力；伶仃洋上飞架起的港珠澳大桥，如同巨龙飞舞，充满自信。而在闹市街头无忧无虑玩耍的孩童，公园里锻炼身体颐养天年的老人，胼手胝足却依然笑对生活的蓝领工人……那一张张安详从容、自由自在的笑脸，构成一卷卷动人的图画，让澳门温馨优雅和睦的生活定格。

关山初度，前路犹长。实现中华民族伟大复兴的美好画卷正在徐徐展开，澳门正大有可为。对澳门来讲，"一国两制"是最大优势，改革开放是最大舞台。坚守"一国"之本，善用"两制"之利，把握国家所需，发挥澳门所长，助力国家全面开放，融入国家发展大局，未来的澳门，宏图在前。

濠江风采满眼春，扬帆破浪正其时。在中央政府的大力支持和澳门特区政府与社会各界的共同努力下，借助粤港澳大湾区的强劲东风，借助共建"一带一路"的重大机遇，澳门的前景一定和我们伟大祖国的前景一样，会越来越好。

澳门，祖国为你骄傲，祖国向你祝福。再过一个20年，你一定会更加美好，更加辉煌！

Two decades ago, in response to the deep-felt call of hundreds of millions of Chinese people, Macao successfully returned to the motherland. The Five-Starred Red Flag and Macao SAR Flag with a lotus flower fluttered in the sea breeze under the blue sky of Macao.

Two decades later, Macao enjoys the care and warmth of the motherland, feeling ineffably happy. In those two decades, Macao people have had a growing sense of identity and of belonging to the motherland, and shown greater love for the motherland and Macao. Macao is no longer a wanderer in a foreign land, but a member of the great Chinese family.

Depending on the motherland and facing the world, Macao has created one economic miracle after another, demonstrating the strong vitality and great superiority of the principle of "one country, two systems." The small town by the Haojiang River has grown into a metropolis. The high sightseeing tower on the sea is full of vitality under the sun; the Hong Kong-Zhuhai-Macao Bridge over the Lingding Sea is like a huge dragon full of confidence. The leisurely and free smiling faces of the children playing in the streets, elders taking exercises in the park and the hard-working blue-collar workers form a touching picture, showing the warm, elegant and harmonious life in Macao.

However, there is still a long way to go. The beautiful picture of realizing the great rejuvenation of the Chinese nation is slowly unfolding. Macao has bright prospects. As for Macao, the principle of "one country, two systems" is the biggest advantage, and the reform and opening up provides the largest stage. Following this principle and bringing its own advantages into play to meet the national needs and contribute to its all-round opening up by integrating into the overall development of the country, Macao sees grand prospects.

By the flowing waters of the Haojiang River, full of spring scenes, Macao is developing at full tilt. With the support of the Central Government and the joint efforts of the SAR government and all sectors in Macao, it will have ever-improving prospects in our great motherland, since the Guangdong-Hong Kong-Macao Greater Bay Area is undergoing vigorous development and the Belt and Road Initiative is bringing major opportunities.

Macao, the motherland is proud of you, and blesses you. In another two decades, you must be more beautiful and prosperous than ever before.

澳门科学馆
Macao Science Center

旅游塔
Macao Tower.

164 莲花盛开 BLOOMING LOTUS FLOWER

澳门街景
Street view of Macao.

新葡京酒店
Grand Lisboa.

第五章 凝心聚力 续谱新篇
V. Making Joint Efforts to Write a New Chapter

澳门最热门的景点之一——威尼斯人酒店,三楼的人造威尼斯运河及天空几乎可以乱真。
The man-made Venice Canal and sky on the third floor of the Venetian Macao, one of Macao's hottest tourist attractions, are almost untrue.

澳门街景
Street view of Macao

井然有序的澳门街头。
Orderly streets in Macao.

170 莲花盛开
BLOOMING LOTUS FLOWER

澳门码头
A Macao wharf.

BLOOMING LOTUS FLOWER
20th Anniversary of Macao's Return

Written by Wang Lingxi   Translated by Zhong Lisha

Publisher: Yu jiutao
Project Coordinator: Fang Yunzhong
Executive Planner: Wang Hui
Specially Invited Editors: Sun Enguang Liang Shusen Ma Zhiyi
Editor: Liu Xiaoxue
Chinese Language Consultant: Wang Yanming
English Editors: Wang Guozhen, Chenxu
English Language Consultant: Michael Geoffrey Murray
English Proofreader: Zhu Luxi
Designer: Zhao Yanchao
Printing Director: Jiao Yang

ISBN 978-7-5146-1834-1